# TO
# FLY
# LIKE
# *A BIRD*

# TO FLY
# LIKE A BIRD

## THE STORY OF MAN-POWERED AIRCRAFT

*KEITH SHERWIN*

BAILEY BROTHERS & SWINFEN LIMITED
**Folkestone**

Distributed by
STERLING PUBLISHING CO., INC.
419 Park Avenue South
New York, N. Y. 10016

*Published in Great Britain by*
*Bailey Brothers and Swinfen Ltd.*

SBN 561 00283 5

*Printed in Great Britain by Clarke, Doble & Brendon, Ltd.*
*Plymouth*

*To Ann*

# Contents

The author at the controls of *Liverpuffin*. *Liverpool Daily Post and Echo*

# Preface

When it comes to discussing man-powered flight, people seem to fall into one of four categories: those who are not interested, those who are interested but know little about it, those who have read a couple of articles in a Sunday Supplement and therefore know all about it, and those who have actually read my previous book on the subject.

Fortunately the first category is very limited as the idea of man-powered · flight inspires an interest that cuts through artificial or intellectual barriers, representing as it does the realisation of one of man's wildest dreams. It is hoped that this book will stimulate this interest in man-powered flight and show that the realisation is worthy of the dream.

The need for a general book of this nature became apparent from the response to my previous book 'Man-Powered Flight'. Although a few of the broader aspects of man-powered flight were mentioned, 'Man-Powered Flight' concentrated largely on the problems involved in man-powered aircraft design.

Through the publication of the previous book many people

have been kind enough to write to me with details of concepts that I would otherwise have missed. One such person was the pioneer Franz Villinger, who supplied additional details and photographs of the 'Mufli' man-powered aircraft.

I wish to thank Philip Green, John McMasters, Josef Malliga, Ron Moulton, Tony Paxton, Dan Perkins, John Potter, Fred To and Peter Wright for the valuable time they have devoted to discussions, without which much of this book could not have been written.

Finally I wish to dedicate this book to my wife as a small tribute to her help and encouragement during its preparation, particularly as she tolerated my hesitant typing throughout much of a rather damp caravan holiday in Scotland.

Keith Sherwin.

# 1

# Man-powered flight

The idea of man flying by using his own human power alone is probably as old as man's wish to conquer an element that has hitherto been the domain of birds. Since this idea is so well established it would appear to be unnecessary to describe what is meant by man-powered flight. Unfortunately this is not the case, because both practical and impractical attempts tend to be indiscriminately considered of equal relevance. At one extreme 'birdmen' who strap small wings to their arms and flap them madly are always destined to failure, yet their attempts are generally portrayed by the mass media as being one aspect of man-powered flight.

The reason for their failure is quite simple. The weight of the man must be supported by lift from the wings in order to fly, and since the lift is related to the size of the wings and the man's speed, the smaller the wings the greater the speed. Such 'birdmen' would need to run at over 60 m.p.h., given ordinary wind conditions, in order to generate sufficient lift for take-off, which is of course impracticable even assuming that their arms were strong enough in the first place to support the loads.

Apart from the impractical aspects of the subject, man-powered flight is such a broadly based activity that it is difficult to give a valid definition that is sufficiently general. At its simplest level the basic requirement is that take-off must be accomplished using human power alone, but this is inadequate as a definition. A high jumper can comply with this requirement, yet by no stretch of the imagination could he be considered to be flying. The simplest form of aircraft to comply with this requirement is a hang-glider, and in the United States, where there is a revival of interest in hang-gliding at the present time, this very broad view of man-powered flight is considered as valid. In Britain and elsewhere in the world only that form of flying where both take-off and propulsion during flight utilise human power is considered to be true man-powered flight. For the purpose of this book it is proposed to avoid any confusion by accepting that hang-gliding and man-powered flight are closely related yet separate branches of aviation. This is not a question of 'splitting hairs', because at the present time there is a fundamental difference between the two activities. With even the simplest man-powered aircraft care must be exercised to ensure a good aerodynamic performance which when combined with a lightweight structure ensures that the required power levels are within the pilot's capabilities. Defining aerodynamic performance in simple terms such as the lift/drag ratio of the aircraft (L/D), this would need to be a minimum of 30 for man-powered aircraft whilst some hang-gliders have an equivalent ratio of only 4. The L/D ratio equals the glide angle so that a hang-glider will only move forward some 4 feet for each foot drop in height, and flights are made as the result of loss of altitude when the glider is launched from a hill top.

The design and construction problems involved with hang-gliders are of a much simpler order than those of man-powered aircraft and it is this that constitutes the major difference between the two. Nevertheless it is proposed to discuss the modern developments of hang-gliders in Chapter 2 since this activity is related to man-powered flight. Future developments may provide that these activities become even more closely related as there are plans to improve the performance of hang-gliders by the incorporation of man-powered propulsion, whilst it is foreseen that man-powered aircraft may utilise help from the atmosphere in the form of up-currents to extend performance. Even without these developments the feed-back of information from each activity may be of direct value to the other.

Taking man-powered flight to embrace both human-powered take-off and propulsion it is perhaps relevant to ask why anybody should wish to exert himself in this manner when other forms of flying have reached such a high level of sophistication. Why this present interest in, and, in many cases, a desire to participate in man-powered flight? The stock answer that mountaineers give when asked why they want to climb a particular mountain is 'because it is there', and this is equally valid for man-powered flight. No other branch of aviation can provide quite the same challenge, since in other types of flight the pilot is being flown in an aircraft rather than being an essential part of the machine. The pilot of a normal aircraft could well be replaced by a computer or some other inanimate object and his function still be performed, but obviously by definition this cannot apply to man-powered flight. Even with gliding, where the pilot needs to use all his skill to extend the performance of his machine by utilising help from the surrounding atmosphere, one cannot have the same rapport with either the machine or the surrounding air as one does with man-powered flight. This may be discarded as being an invalid argument on the grounds that it is too emotional, but emotions do play a very big part in any such activity. Enea Bossi, designer of the "Pedaliante" man-powered aircraft that flew in 1936, wrote in the early

3

sixties 'to the man that will design an aerocycle, that at the breathtaking moment when he sees the plane a few inches off the ground for a few seconds, he will never forget those seconds for the rest of his life'.

In the case of Enea Bossi his was a particularly long life. He died in 1964 at the age of 76, so that these words best convey the satisfaction to be gained from such an activity whether participating as designer or pilot. However, since most of us live in an essentially practical environment, there must be more 'down to earth' reasons for the continuation and furtherance of any activity.

It is generally recognised that any aeronautical activity cannot develop rapidly unless it has a military objective. Certainly one cannot foresee any military aim for man-powered aircraft so that there is small likelihood of high capital investment. Fortunately however, it is possible to develop man-powered flight on low budgets and there is sufficient interest in the subject to anticipate progress for the reasons listed below:-

(1) It is still at the pioneering stage where private individuals can participate without the need of elaborate materials or manufacturing facilities and without any financial burden other than that normally associated with a hobby. Furthermore, as a pioneering activity man-powered flight is still at the stage where individuals can make appreciable contributions to its development.

(2) The design and/or construction of a man-powered aircraft makes an excellent student project and is a valuable education tool. Chapter 6 describes such a project in detail, including the reasons for its initial choice.

(3) One aim of man-powered flight is the winning of the Kremer prizes. There are two prizes of £50,000 and £5,000 respectively, the rules of the two competitions being described towards the end of this chapter.

(4) Man-powered flight has the potential to be developed into a sport, possibly along similar lines to gliding. It must

be remembered that the pioneering stage of gliding up to the early 1920's gave no indication of its true potential or of the major developments that resulted. The idea of man-powered flight as a sport is explored in more detail in Chapter 7.

(5) The need to solve many new problems together with the creative freedom within any such pioneering activity should ensure that man-powered flight provides new technological developments of value to other branches of aviation and to engineering as a whole. Also, as gliding added to the meterologist's knowledge of the atmosphere, so man-powered flight may add to our knowledge regarding its behaviour at very low altitudes.

Whatever the reasons are for a personal interest in man-powered flight there have been sufficient developments in low speed aerodynamics and in lightweight structures at the present time to have allowed the building and flying of several man-powered aircraft. The purpose of this book is to describe these developments and the aircraft within which they have been incorporated to indicate that man-powered flight is essentially a practical activity that could become an accepted branch of aviation.

Legend has it that Icarus was the first person to attempt man-powered flight. The story goes that King Minos imprisoned the engineer Daedalus and his son Icarus in the Labyrinth in his palace at Knossos on Crete. Daedalus constructed wings for Icarus with strict instructions that on flying to safety he was not to fly too high otherwise the glue would melt. The details of the structure vary with the different recorded versions of the legend, the most popular being a wing form with feathers attached to the hero's arms by means of glue or wax. Whatever the structure the story indicates that Icarus disregarded this advice and soared too high whereupon the glue melted. Icarus fell into the sea and perished.

This legend is of course extremely well known and is

probably one of the reasons that the concept of man-powered flight is both accepted and understood today. Perhaps in some ways this is unfortunate as many people still think of man-powered flight in terms of flapping wings and therefore of being impractical. Also, the other widely accepted view of this legend is as a warning to mankind not to take too great a leap into the unknown. To quote Michael Ayrton in his "The Testament of Daedalus":-

'The myth of Daedalus and Icarus has something in common with that other great symbolic myth of Prometheus. To venture innovation is to offend. To raise man up to civilization from the apelike condition to which he was called is to invite the retribution of the conservative and stabilizing powers of heaven. To cross the barrier of earth and spread wings in a different element is to break the natural law and must call for punishment. And yet we know that it is also man's nature and excellence to break the rules. Life is impossible without revolution.

The abiding strength and value of these myths is in the fact that both opposites are true. Change is admirable, but a substratum of permanence is essential. An excess of motion will lead to disintegration; a persistent stability must end in a return from life to the mineral state'.

This expresses a point of view that is wide-spread but not necessarily relevant to engineering, and it is engineering that is concerned in this case. Daedalus represents an engineer and it is engineering that allows great technological steps to reach practical reality. That aspect of engineering which is concerned with translating defined aims into end products is design, a process that is very difficult to define but nevertheless is a process that all engineers must be concerned with in order to achieve anything. The disciplines involved in design require that engineers must innovate, or be creative, in order to ensure that the best solution to a problem is found. Once having one or more solutions the engineer then has to ensure that it, or they, work in practice. This is the main difference between engineers and inventors since the latter do not necessarily check on the validity of their ideas. A 'crank' is one who seizes an idea and builds a device on the basis of that idea without checking that such a device is practicable. Engineers check the validity of a proposed design either through their experience, and if this is incomplete by using scientific principles to set up a theoretical model of the problem, or, more commonly, by experimentation.

This approach to a problem is discussed here because it is of direct relevance to the design of man-powered aircraft. There is room for, and a need for, innovation in man-powered flight, but this must be tempered by practical considerations in order that the time and money expended on such an activity are not wasted and, even more important, that the concept is not brought into disrepute. Fortunately there is sufficient experience and knowledge available to ensure success, some of the basic information being presented within this book.

Stripping the embellishments of legend away one wonders whether the story of Icarus is a record of an attempt by an earlier 'crank' or whether it has some greater significance. The idea of a man rising rapidly upwards and then suddenly falling, even though it is confused by the idea of the glue melting in the sun's heat, is a typical description of a stall. Such legends do generally tend to have some basis of truth and mark important events in the life of the people. The achieving of flight by a man would of course be a very important event. The Minoan civilisation had highly skilled craftsmen who, combining their skill with the genius of their engineers, could have enabled the flights to take place some three thousand years before the accepted pioneers in aviation were born. Whether such a flight occurred we shall probably never know but certainly the basic ideas of aerodynamics are in fact related to and are no more difficult to understand than the concepts of hydraulics with which the Minoans were familiar. Also the Minoans were closely linked through both culture and trade to Egypt, and within recent years there have been some discoveries indicating that flying machines may have been built in ancient Egypt. This is a most interesting development as the Egyptians tended to record all events whereas the Minoans recorded only items of social or commercial importance.

The next record of any development in man-powered flight was by Leonardo da Vinci who not only made an intense study of bird flight and wing motion, but extended these ideas to the design of a man-powered ornithopter. There is no record of a man-carrying model having been constructed and even if it had been it is doubtful whether it would have flown. Since the wings of an ornithopter have to provide both lift and propulsion the flapping motion is quite complex and even with today's knowledge we are a long way from defining the physical rules necessary for the design of such a machine. However, the approach of da Vinci was basically sound within the confines of the limited aeronautical knowledge of the time, since it was perhaps logical that with limited power it should be used to provide lift directly. He designed not only an ornithopter but also a helicopter, and in doing so fell into the trap in which many subsequent investigators also found themselves — that of not realising that lift can be obtained from a fixed plane. This is rather surprising in one respect since a kite is the simplest form of fixed lifting plane and had been invented by the Chinese.

Progress towards practical flight was slow until the eighteenth century when Sir George Cayley, rightfully acknowledged as the father of British aviation, utilised the principle of the lifting plane to build the first man-carrying glider in the early 1850's. Cayley was born at Scarborough on 27 December 1773. His mother fortunately encouraged his lively curiosity and so laid the foundations for his life of research and investigation. Cayley succeeded to the title as sixth Baronet in 1792 and three years later married the daughter of his former tutor, George Walker F.R.S. This marriage provided the necessary stability for his various aeronautical activities.

As early as 1804 Cayley built a model glider that flew successfully. He wrote that "It was very pretty to see it sail down a steep hill, and it gave the idea that a larger instrument would be a better and a safer conveyance down the Alps than even the sure-footed mule, let him meditate his track ever so intensely".

Further developments were inspired by reports that in Vienna Jacob Degen had flown briefly, using wings by means of his own muscle power. However, it was not recorded that most of Degen's weight was supported by a balloon and that by flapping his wings he was able to make extended jumps of several yards.

Inspired by Degen's supposed achievement Cayley continued to make larger gliders. By 1809 he produced one of 300 square feet surface of which he wrote "When any person ran forward in it, with his full speed, taking advantage of a gentle breeze in front, it would bear upward so strongly as scarcely to allow him to touch the ground; and would frequently lift him up, and convey him several yards together".

Although this was the first account of a full sized aeroplane, the first true man-carrying flight was not till 1853 when Cayley's unwilling coachman made a flight across the dale at Brompton. An eye-witness recorded that the coachman got himself clear after the flight and shouted "Please, Sir George, I wish to give notice. I was hired to drive, and not to fly. . . ."

The configuration of Cayley's man-carrying glider, his "new flyer" as he termed it, is shown in Figure 1. A full size replica was made and flown in 1973 with Derek Piggott as the pilot. Derek Piggott is the Chief Flying Instructor at Larham Gliding Club and he is well known not only for his achievement within aviation but for his willingness to participate in pioneering activities. He made the first true man-powered flight in Britain with the Southampton machine and this is described in Chapter 3.

9

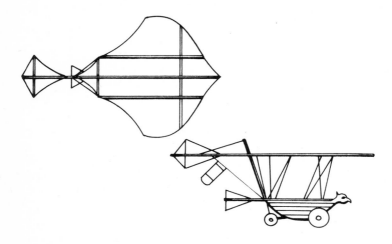

*Figure 1.* Configuration of the *Cayley* man-carrying glider.

One incident concerning Derek Piggott recorded by Michael Cumming in his book on gliding entitled 'Powerless Ones' is of particular interest. It concerns a Slingsby Sedbergh open 2 seater training glider that was entered by the Home Command Gliding Instructors school of the A.T.C. for the 1953 National Gliding Championships. This was held at Great Hucklow in Derbyshire.

Compared to the high performance gliders of the other competitors the Sedbergh was a bit of a joke, because it was open, had no all-weather equipment or oxygen, and had a very much lower performance. Nevertheless it was launched on the second day into uncertain weather with Derek Piggott, then a flight Lieutenant, as the pilot and a cadet as co-pilot, and went on to achieve a 15,240 ft. gain-of-height record, a height of 2,490 ft. in excess of the previous British and National record.

What happened was that they entered a cumulo-nimbus

cloud and climbed up inside before leaving at a level of 16-17,000 ft. At that level the temperature is down to about -4° F and they were in an open cockpit. The aircraft and crew were covered with ice and they were flying without oxygen, which is considered a necessity at 15,000 ft., otherwise the pilot's efficiency is impaired. On the glide down they were troubled by ice breaking off the nose of the glider and sliding backwards, as neither crew members were protected. The cadet had been troubled by the cold and by vomiting, which is normal at a high altitude. He was also troubled by loss of feeling in his legs and was suffering from exposure. Apparently Piggott was untroubled by either cold or height. On landing he ran, actually ran, for help.

Before leaving this discussion of Cayley's aeronautical activities it is of note that his 300 sq. ft. glider of 1809 crashed with a boy on board during experiments being carried out regarding aircraft propulsion using flapping wings, as a result of which Cayley concluded that man-powered flight was not a practical proposition at least within the limitations of the then 'state of the art'.

After Cayley, aeronautical activities increased in number although not necessarily in success. The next experimenter of note was Otto Lilienthal, the German who is considered to be the first person to achieve practical gliding flight, making over one thousand flights before losing his life in a flying accident in 1896. Although, historically, Lilienthal is remembered for his pioneering work in aeronautics and for stimulating the interest of the Wright brothers, with the well-known result, his work has direct relevance today in the field of hang-gliding. He initiated hang-gliding as a practical form of control at a time when aviation was in its infancy and the primary problem was one of just flying, with control being relegated to second place. The mechanism of control was by the pilot hanging below the glider and swinging his body in order to change the centre of gravity of the machine. This also allowed the pilot's legs to act as the undercarriage and provide direct

11

drive for the take-off run. Lilienthal's first approach to flying was from a springboard set up in his garden. This allowed him to gain initial experience but he realised that most help could be gained from taking-off into wind, so he had a conical hill built near Grosskreuz. It was 50 ft high and from it he could launch into wind regardless of direction. The main problem was that Lilienthal's gliders had low weight in order that the take-off speed was sufficiently low to be accomplished by the pilot's running. This resulted in machines that were difficult to handle on the ground particularly in a wind, a problem that is still relevant today with man-powered aircraft.

The history of Lilienthal's approach to gliding is covered in more detail by Ann and Lorne Welch in their book "The Story of Gliding" as also is the subsequent history of gliding. No further details will be provided as it is outside the scope of this book. Sufficient to say that the work of Lilienthal inspired others, chief amongst them being the Wright brothers who made the first powered flight in 1903. Although gliding continued it was of secondary importance to powered flying until after the first world war. At the end of the war the Treaty of Versailles imposed strict limitations on aviation in Germany. No powered aircraft were to be built or imported, but fortunately no restriction was placed on gliding. Post-war development of gliding within Germany was initiated by Oscar Ursinus, editor of the German magazine 'Flugsport'. He organised meetings at the Wasserkuppe, a hill of some 3000 ft. height in the Rhon-Gerbirge area of central Germany. The first Rhon meeting of 1920 produced considerable interest but a maximum flight of only 2¼ minutes' duration. These early flights inspired design and development of gliders within Germany to the extent that by the 1922 meeting soaring techniques were enabling flights of several hours to be made. These successes at the Wasserkuppe led eventually to utilising thermals and cross-country flights with gliders that were robust and manœuvrable as well as having good aerodynamic performance.

It is perhaps not surprising that the first serious attempts at man-powered flight should have been carried out in Germany, again inspired by Oscar Ursinus. Prior to these there had been many attempts at trying to get man into the air under his own power. The earliest attempts of note were in France where simple wings were attached to bicycles to gain speed for take-off. A competition was sponsored by the firm of Peugeot in 1913 when a prize of 10,000 francs was offered for a flight of 10 metres over level ground with such a machine. When it became apparent that this task was too difficult, a preliminary prize of 1,000 francs was offered for a 'flight' of one metre at a minimum height of 1/10 metre, but unfortunately even this was not attained.

In the United States a six-winged aircraft, the Gerhardt Hexaplane, was built in order to achieve man-powered flight.

*The Gerhardt Hexaplane* built in 1923. *Smithsonian Institution*

13

Having a wingspan of 40 ft. and a height of 19 ft. for an empty weight of only 100 lb. it was too fragile, and the wings collapsed after a short 'hop' 3 inches above the ground. It has been described as a 'venetian blind' and just like its namesake it folded up. Many such impractical projects were also taking place in Germany so the inventors were invited to the Wasserkuppe in order that their knowledge could be shared and they could learn from the gliders flying from there. One such participant was a medical doctor, Dr. Brustmann, who had a type of ornithopter built around a bicycle. This did not fly, but the information passed on by Dr. Brustmann was of direct relevance to man-powered flight. He trained atheletes for Olympic competitions and had measured the power output for trained sportsmen indicating that they could produce up to 2 h.p. for very short periods. Although we know that this data was too optimistic it inspired a scientifically based study of man-powered flight. It was quickly realised that a lightweight glider plus pilot would absorb about 1 h.p. in level flight and therefore short man-powered flights were feasible.

Dr. Lippisch, who had already achieved fame through the

An *Ornithopter* designed by Dr. Alexander Lippisch, flown in 1929. *Dr. Lippisch*

design of such successful gliders as the 'Professor' and 'Wien', designed a man-powered ornithopter, the flapping wing approach still being favoured at that time. It was reasoned that this was best suited to the action of muscles and gave promise of a higher efficiency than a conventional propeller drive together with lower structural weight. The Lippisch ornithopter incorporated a high wing layout of 38 ft. span with an open pilot seat and covered fuselage behind it. The wings were moved by the action of the legs in a movement similar to that used in rowing. Control of the machine was by stick for rudder and elevator. There were no ailerons as it was considered that differential speed of flapping the two wings would give some form of lateral control. The empty weight of the machine was approximately 110lb., a comparatively low weight, particularly in view of the materials of construction available at the time. The wings were made fairly flexible as it was considered that the twisting during the down stroke would help propulsion, although from wind tunnel tests it was fully expected that a good propulsive efficiency could be achieved without twisting. Initial tests showed that the wings did not appear to twist and that there was no appreciable improvement over the normal gliding flight. Lippisch then added small flexible sections to the trailing edges of the wings and these made a considerable difference to the propulsive action.

A young pilot Hans Werner Krause was chosen to fly the ornithopter as he was also a good athlete. The first few flights were disappointing until it was realised that the main trouble was Hans Werner. With irrefutable logic he did not see any real reason for working hard while flying since a small engine could have done the thing so much better. However, Lippisch managed to persuade the pilot to fly the aircraft over a predetermined distance by promising a holiday for Hans Werner to go and see his girl friend in Berlin.

The flight was achieved at the first attempt. A length of 300 yards was proposed from a shock cord launch and the course was marked by a small puddle that had to be crossed at the end of the flight. To the onlookers' amazement and amusement Hans Werner Krause crossed the 'lake' in flapping flight, and he was on his way to the railway station within 10 minutes of landing. Unfortunately the aircraft was afterwards sent to Berlin for an exhibition and a steel undercarriage was added for improved take-offs that kept it firmly earthbound.

At best the Lippisch ornithopter could only be counted as achieving a man-assisted flight, but nevertheless it clearly showed the possibilities of man-powered flight. More recently Dr. Lippisch expressed the view that the flapping wing propulsion still has great potential especially as a non-stationary wing modifies the flow around a wing, improving performance in gliding. Since the Lippisch ornithopter flew in 1929 later experiments show that rather than have the whole wings moving it would have been better to have a fixed centre wing section with flapping parts only at the outer portions. Furthermore a rotational flapping motion similar to the wing movement of insects and birds is far more efficient than the simple up and down movement of the Lippisch ornithopter. Even without these later improvements the Lippisch machine is still the most successful known ornithopter to have flown to date.

Following these early flights in Germany, Oscar Ursinus arranged for The Polytechnische Gesellschaft of Frankfurt to offer a prize of 500 marks for a man-powered flight round two pylons set 500 metres apart, the flight being more than 1 km. in length. Storage of energy for take-off was permitted in the form of a rubber catapult provided that an equivalent weight of 20 lb. was carried aboard the aircraft. Only one aircraft was built in Germany to enter this competition, the Haessler-Villinger machine. Helmut Haessler and Frank Villinger were two engineers with Junkers, and started design and construction of their machine, which they named "Mufli", in 1935. The first flight was on 29th August, 1935, at Frankfurt airport when the aircraft climbed to 10 feet altitude, at

*The Haessler-Villinger Mulfi* man-powered aircraft flown in 1935.

Photograph showing pilot access to aircraft. *Franz Villinger*

which height the pilot used his power to fly horizontally for a distance of about 400 ft. Take-off was accomplished by the pilot anchoring the aircraft, stretching rubber cables from the aircraft to a second anchor point then releasing the aircraft anchor from inside the fuselage.

The Haessler-Villinger machine made a total of 120 flights from catapult launches between 1935 and February 1938, when it was given to the Luftfahrt Museum at Berlin. Unfortunately it was destroyed during the Second World War, but Haessler presented comprehensive details of the project to the Canadian Aeronautical Journal which were published in 1961. Of the flights made 80 were man-powered, the others were for testing changes in trim and control and for pilot training. A maximum distance of 790 yards was achieved on 4th July, 1937, for which a consolation prize was given even though the original competition was not won.

Design of the machine was based on values of man-power measured by Haessler as early as 1933, the method of testing was by having the person being tested ride a cycle towing another cyclist of the same weight and in the same riding position; tension in the towing cable was measured, and the time taken to cover a given distance. From these the power to move the second cyclist could be worked out, the total power of the cyclists being measured equalling twice this amount. From these tests a cyclist was found to have a power output of 1.3 h.p. for 30 seconds. The design started using this data but when it became certain that the weight of 20 lb. had to be incorporated the competition was out of the question and the aircraft continued on the basis of achieving horizontal man-powered flight. The original cyclist was given flying instruction but proved unsuitable so a first pilot was chosen on his flying skill although his power output was approximately 40% lower than originally hoped for. This indicates the sound design reasoning behind the Haessler-Villinger machine since it made aeronautical history and proved the feasibility of man-powered flight with a lower power output.

The aircraft had a wingspan of 45 ft., which was normal for high performance gliders of the period, but the empty weight was only 80 lb. although an additional 20 lb. had to be carried as well. To save weight the conventional controls were not used, the angle of attack of the wing being altered by the pilot instead. The two wing half angles were changed differentially for lateral control and together for longitudinal control. This was not satisfactory in practice as it resulted in over controlled take-offs with too steep a climb, so that in 1936 this was changed to the more usual elevator arrangement which gave better results. The pilot operated the controls with his hands whilst pedalling in a reclining position, the drive being taken from the pedals to a propeller mounted on a pylon above the pilot by means of a twisted belt. Special flat belts were developed with a rubberised surface to minimise slip and the pulleys used also had rubberised surfaces for the same reason. With the belting materials then available some stretching was experienced so the belts had to be changed every six flights. Today with materials like nylon this would be unnecessary, but this clearly indicates the disadvantages under which pioneers like Haessler and Villinger had to work.

In the 1960's Haessler proposed an improved version of this basic design with an increased wingspan of 82 ft. and with a driven undercarriage which he estimated would be capable of flights of up to an hour based on an empty weight of 110 lb. and pilot weight of between 132 and 140 lb. Unfortunately this remained only a proposal, being designated as the H4, but from subsequent man-powered aircraft we can only conclude that these performance estimates were too optimistic.

Whilst these German developments were taking place a prize equivalent to £5,000 was offered by the Italian Government for a flight of 1 kilometre, using human power. Only one machine was built to attempt this competition – the "Pedaliante" designed by Enea Bossi and constructed with the help of his friend Vittorio Bonomi. The words quoted earlier by Enea Bossi contained a reference to a man-powered aircraft as an 'aerocycle' which is a literal translation of 'Pedaliante' which means more generally 'fly by pedals'.

Bossi had been studying the possibility of man-powered flight previous to the offer of the prize, after having his interest stimulated when reading that a man claimed to have built and flown an aircraft equipped with a 1 h.p. motor in 1935. This report inspired him to check the feasibility of such a design and to become interested in man-powered flight where the power levels are similar. Since his primary problem was similar to that of Haessler, that of obtaining reliable data

The *Bossi-Bonomi Pedaliante* flown in 1936.

on the performance of man, he carried out tests to rectify this position. The first tests represented a practical but nevertheless fascinating approach to the problem, since Bossi had a cyclist tow a glider into the air. For these a well designed primary glider, a type of glider of simple open construction with the pilot sitting in the open, was used with a very light pilot. Several flights made at heights of 2 or 3 ft. above the ground got distances up to 300 yards, the longest flight being terminated by the glider striking a pole at the side of the road.

These tests proved the feasibility of man-powered flight but it was noted that the performance varied noticeably according to the physical condition of the cyclist and the atmosphere, wind and temperature. The bicycle for these tests was geared to have a maximum speed of 25 m.p.h. and from measuring the tension in the tow rope it was concluded that the cyclist could produce up to 1.27 h.p. for more than a minute. The 'Pedaliante' aircraft was designed to come well within this power limitation. Further tests were then carried out by replacing the chain of the bicycle with an equivalent drive to a single propeller mounted behind the cycle. A maximum speed of 23 m.p.h. was achieved but this limit was imposed by the gyroscopic action of the propeller making the cycle unmanageable. From these tests Bossi decided that two propellers were necessary to overcome the gyroscopic effect, a conclusion which in the light of subsequent experience was proved to be invalid, as the effect is considerably reduced when applied to a larger structure such as an aircraft.

The 'Pedaliante' aircraft was a monoplane of 56 ft. wing-span, the monoplane layout being chosen in preference to a biplane as it was considered that at the low speeds it would fly at, 20 to 23 m.p.h., the difference in drag between the two layouts was unimportant, and that the lower weight of the monoplane was the biggest factor. Originally the aircraft was designed for a safety factor of 2 which gave a weight of 160 lb., this being chosen as the low speeds and heights at which it was anticipated the aircraft would fly constituted no serious risk to the pilot. However, the Italian authorities had other ideas and would not permit the aircraft to fly without the safety factor being increased to nearly twice that originally assumed, thereby increasing the weight to 220 lb. It was realised that this increase of 60 lb. would jeopardise the success of the project in terms of winning the prize but the project went ahead and Bossi spent about the equivalent of $12,000 on having his machine built.

The first flight took place in 1936 when in Bossi's own words 'the plane actually took off by its own power, and flew 300 ft. before landing'. Bossi's actual words are quoted because this statement has caused more controversy than perhaps any other statement regarding man-powered flight. The main problem has been the long time period between the deed and the report on this project presented in 1961. It has been argued that Bossi was an old man when he wrote this and that his memory was not what it should have been. Evidence to support this view was obtained from others connected with the project and the general consensus of opinion has been not to accept the Bossi view of the flight. However, without wishing to prolong a rather fruitless argument, there is really no logical reason for disbelieving Bossi's account of the flight as it would be such a momentous event in his life that he would be unlikely to forget the details of such a flight.

Furthermore, again without trying to cast any doubt on evidence, the witnesses of such a flight could presumably suffer from the same faults of memory as it was assumed Bossi had. On the technical side the 'Pedaliante' was equipped with a driven undercarriage and so was capable of man-powered take-offs. Power required for take-off is estimated as being of the order of 0.9 h.p. which was within the capabilities of the pilot, especially if some help was gained from the atmosphere in the form of a head wind or alternatively by up-currents. In fact this must have been the case because of 43 flights, only the first is claimed to have had a man-powered take-off, the others being achieved only from cata-pult launches. The best flight was of 980 yards but apparently this was achieved at the expense of considerable loss of altitude. To improve performance, Bossi redesigned the pro-pellers several times increasing diameter each time and thereby gaining an increase in thrust until maximum diameter was reached, with the propellers nearly touching the fuselage. However, the extra 60 lb. weight of the airframe was the real cause of poor performance and without this limitation one can only speculate as to the flights the 'Pedaliante' would have achieved and so inspired even more rapid development in man-powered flight.

Unfortunately any developments that could have arisen were halted by the Second World War during which the 'Pedaliante' was destroyed. The general problem of man-powered flight was shelved until after the war, when in 1948 B. Worley published an article indicating better performances if full advantage were taken of the then latest knowledge of design. This was also the basic theme of a later article pub-lished in 1953 by August Raspet who actually proposed the aircraft configuration shown in Figure 2. This design had a

22

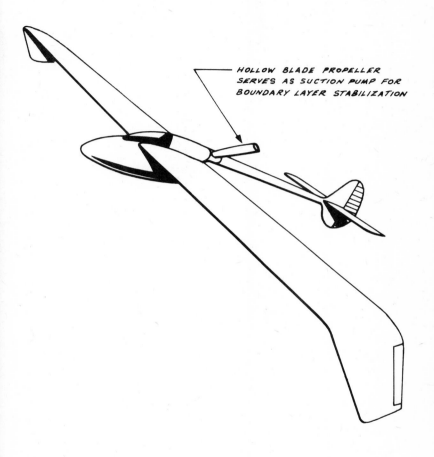

HOLLOW BLADE PROPELLER
SERVES AS SUCTION PUMP FOR
BOUNDARY LAYER STABILIZATION

*Figure 2.* Proposed design of man-powered aircraft by Raspet.

wingspan and chord of 40 and 5 ft. respectively which with an estimated weight of 300 lb. would have a flying speed of 18 m.p.h. The proposed sophistication of boundary layer control over the upper wing surface would have resulted in a very low drag and it was estimated that power requirement for flight near the ground was a mere 0.45 h.p. Unfortunately, as with many other similar design studies, this idea was not translated into practice.

A man-powered aircraft was built in Germany that 'flew' in 1955 with Hans Zacher as the pilot. The only information available on this project comes from the pilot, who was called in to fly the machine because of his connection with gliding. Apparently the configuration was similar to that of the Bossi 'Pedaliante' but the construction was both weak and poorly executed. It had a driven undercarriage and during the take-off run part of the drive assembly structure broke, but the pilot just managed to get it into the air and then glide for a short distance.

Following these developments the real post-war effort had to wait until 1956 when in Britain T.R.F. Nonweiler, a lecturer at the College of Aeronautics, later to become Professor of Aeronautics at Glasgow University, and B.S. Shenstone, then Chief Engineer of B.E.A., started writing and talking about man-powered flight almost simultaneously. At about the same time Dan Perkins, a civil servant at the Cardington Balloon establishment built the first of his man-powered aircraft with inflatable wings. This constructional approach stemmed from his experience with inflatable structures and from the realisation that success in man-powered flight rested on the use of lightweight aircraft.

He joined Cardington in 1938 and since then has worked not only on balloons but also many other devices including an inflatable bridge capable of supporting a 6 ton truck. Man-powered flight inspired him as he was convinced that it provided the opportunity for 'aviation for the million', provided that inflatable structures were employed. His aim was a simple, lightweight aircraft that could be carried in the boot of a car and that anybody could own. Dan Perkins is also careful to point out that an inflatable aircraft is extremely safe in the unlikely event of a collision.

Perkins' first machine had a wing of 100 sq. ft. area with an aspect ratio — span over the chord — of 15 whereas previous inflatable wings had aspect ratios no greater than 3½. A symmetrical aerofoil of thickness/chord ratio of 20% was used in the wing and was braced by wire from the fuselage for improved strength. The total weight of the machine was about 220 lb. of which the aircraft empty weight represented 62 lb. It was estimated that the power required for take-off was within the pilot's capability. Take-off speed should have been of the order of 20 m.p.h. but during tests with Perkins as the pilot a speed of only 14 m.p.h. was developed.

Using the same wing Perkins then redesigned the aircraft twice more in order to improve performance. The second machine had a fully streamlined fuselage with the pilot changed from a normal cycling to a semi-reclining position, thereby reducing the frontal area of the fuselage from 15 to 5 sq. ft. The propeller was moved to a forward 'tractor' position and this was balanced by a butterfly tail.

As the second aircraft still did not perform as expected a third aircraft was built with a canard configuration — that is, tail first. In order to make the taxi-ing trials Dan Perkins used to take advantage of calm periods in the early morning or at dusk. He recalls getting up at 4 o'clock one morning to attempt a flight only to find at the airfield that the wind strength was too great. He crawled back to bed only to be accused by his wife of going to bed too late.

In view of the disappointing performance with the three aircraft an investigation of the drive was then undertaken to check for lost power. The mechanical drive employed a rubber-proofed rope belt moving over vee pulleys and the complete system had a reasonably high efficiency of 91%. Although slightly lower than the 94-96% expected for most

Perkins' first three aircraft with inflatable wings. All used the same wing but the difference between the first and second was in the design of the fuselage, whilst the third changed to a canard configuration. *Author's collection*

man-powered aircraft drive systems this would not explain the magnitude of the lost power. The propeller was then checked and found to be part of the trouble. Although the propeller had a high efficiency at low forward speeds the efficiency fell as the forward speeds approached 14 m.p.h. since any increase in power input from the pilot simply went into increasing the airspeed of the air entering the propeller without any corresponding increase in thrust. In retrospect Dan Perkins is now convinced that his first aircraft could have flown provided that he had not been 'big-headed' in trying to fly them himself. As he was in his 50's when he attempted to fly them he feels that he should have enlisted the help of a trained cyclist as he did for his successful aircraft.

As the first three of Perkins' aircraft were unsuccessful and as they relied solely on propeller thrust for take-off it was generally concluded that this method of getting airborne was impractical, not only for the Perkins machine but for man-powered aircraft in general. Fortunately this has since been disproved by later man-powered aircraft actually rising from the ground using propeller thrust only, one of them being Perkins' last machine 'Reluctant Phoenix'. Based upon this early experience most man-powered aircraft have subsequently relied on the use of driven undercarriages for power during the take-off run.

No other man-powered aircraft were built during the 1950's although developments continued through the formation of a man-powered aircraft Committee in January, 1957. The original members of this Committee were as follows:

| H. B. Irving | Chairman |
| J. R. Brown | London School of Hygiene and Tropical Medicine. |
| Robert Graham | Microcell Limited |
| Thurston James | Editor of 'The Aeroplane' |
| A. Newell | College of Aeronautics |
| T.R.F. Nonweiler | Queens University of Belfast |
| B.S. Shenstone | British European Airways. |

This Committee eventually became the Man-Powered Aircraft Group of the Royal Aeronautical Society and in this form is still flourishing today. Of the original committee Robert Graham and Thurston James continue to serve as active members of the Group Committee, Robert Graham serving as the Chairman since 1961. By so doing they have ensured the continuity that is necessary for any such organisation and have provided encouragement to man-powered flight developments in Britain. It is also interesting to note that man-powered flight is not the only pioneering aeronautical activity with which Robert Graham has been involved. He was the test pilot for the Brennan helicopter built at the Royal Aircraft Establishment, Farnborough, in 1925. The testing would probably be viewed with some concern in the light of today's strict controls as the machine was unstable and there was a danger that the 60 ft. rota above the pilot's head being driven round by tip mounted propellers could have struck the runway. Although the helicopter did not get very far off the ground it must be remembered that this work was well in advance of Sikorsky's pioneering helicopter developments of the Second World War.

The Man-powered Aircraft Committee initially aimed at being able to assist financially those man-powered aircraft designs that were promising. With this in view a fund was established for which a sum of £5,000 was collected. Whilst this money was being collected Henry Kremer, an industrialist, became interested in the prospect of man-powered flights, spurred on no doubt by his association with Robert Graham. In November 1959 he offered a prize of £5,000 for the first British aircraft to fly under man-power alone, without any help from power storage or buoyant gas devices, around a 'figure of eight' course. The course was to have two turning points not less than ½ mile apart, the aircraft entering the start at an altitude of over 10 ft. and leaving at this same height, the altitude between being unrestricted. Furthermore it was stipulated that the aircraft should be powered and

28

controlled by the crew throughout, only one ground crew member being allowed to assist during take-off. The flight was to take place in still air conditions, which for the purpose was defined as wind not exceeding a speed of 10 knots.

Stemming from the inspiration of the Kremer prize and the financial help of the Group the Southampton and Hatfield man-powered aircraft were built and flew in 1961, these being the first practical man-powered aircraft described in Chapter 3. In all over fifteen known man-powered aircraft have been built and have achieved true flight, that is they have taken off and flown under man-power alone, but none as yet have even attempted the Kremer competition. In 1967 the prize money was doubled to £10,000 and the competition was opened to all nationalities. In addition a further set of prizes totalling £5,000 were offered by Mr. Kremer for a simpler competition open to citizens of the United Kingdom or the British Commonwealth. The course for these prizes consists of two flights in opposite directions of 'slalom' formation along three markers spaced at ¼ mile intervals in a straight line, the two flights to be completed within an hour. Furthermore it is required that the aircraft attain an altitude of 10 ft. when passing the first and third markers on both flights. The prize money, to be split into separate prizes of £2,500, £1,500 and £1,000, was to be awarded to the first three contestants to fulfil these conditions.

In 1973 the prize money for the 'figure of eight' competition was uprated from £10,000 to £50,000 in the hope that it would attract still more positive attempts. At the time of writing it appears unlikely that the Kremer prize will be won before the competition rules come up for review. Whether the rules will be modified or whether the time scale will be extended is uncertain, but the organisers obviously have the difficult job of assessing how effective a competition can be in stimulating interest in man-powered aircraft developments without making it more attainable. At the present time the Kremer competitions are continuing to serve a useful purpose either directly by inspiring the construction of such aircraft as the Malliga and Wright machines, both private ventures described in Chapter 3, or indirectly by providing a public relations image for man-powered flight in general.

# 2

# *Hang-gliding*

Hang-gliding gets its name quite naturally from the position of the pilot, the pilot hanging through or under the machine by his arms or supported by straps, rather than sitting within a fuselage in the conventional manner. More recent developments in hang-gliding have resulted in durations lasting hours instead of seconds. It is impractical to have the pilot hanging by his arms for too long a period. Modern hang-gliders therefore include seats under the wing for supporting the pilot, but the mode of operation is exactly the same.

The pilot's legs are the machine's undercarriage and means of power for take-off so that the method of getting air-borne is apparently to run into wind until the relative airspeed is sufficient to sustain flight, and then at the point of take-off swing one's body about to alter the centre of gravity in order to control the machine in the air. This essentially is what hang-gliding is all about and it was this mode of control that persuaded pioneers like Lilienthal to initiate this form of flying. Obviously flying a hang-glider is not as simple as this description implies, as the pilot needs to co-ordinate all aspects of the flight directly with his own body since this is an essential part of the machine. However, even though effective controls were developed for aircraft, hang-gliding has retained an important place in aviation as it represents the simplest and most inexpensive form of flying available. Furthermore it is reputed to be more exhilarating and give a more intense feeling of being in tune with nature than any other form of flying.

Most hang-glider flying takes place into light or moderate winds of about 15 m.p.h., and since the pilot has to run into wind for take-off this means that the equivalent flying speed of such machines is of the order of 20 m.p.h. Designing hang-gliders for such low air speeds means keeping the overall weight down to a minimum and maintaining a low wing loading by having a relatively large wing area. It would be quite feasible to design hang-gliders with higher flying speeds in order to fly in stronger winds but there would be attendant problems, first of controlling them on the ground and then of making high speed landings with only the pilot's legs between the glider and the stationary ground.

To design and build a hang-glider with a low wing loading at first sight appears to be simply a question of making a sufficiently large wing. However it is not quite as straightforward as this as there are the conflicting requirements of a large wing and a very low weight. A large wing weighs more than a smaller one and involves greater expense and constructional time. To illustrate this with a few simple figures let us compare two typical hang-glider design possibilities, one of 1 lb./sq. ft. and the other of 2 lb./sq. ft. wing loading. If we consider them both for a pilot weighing 150 lb. the characteristics of the two machines can be tabulated as follows:

| Wing loading (lb./sq. ft.) | Wing area (sq. ft.) | Empty weight (lb.) | Speed (m.p.h.) |
|---|---|---|---|
| 1 | 225 | 75 | 20 |
| 2 | 90 | 30 | 28 |

From this example it can be seen that a higher wing loading has several practical advantages, mainly in terms of a smaller machine that is easier to build, store and transport. From the point of view of actually flying, the glider with the lower wing loading has the advantage of the lower air speed. The designers of such machines go for a compromise solution and present day hang-gliders have wing loadings of about 1½ lb/ sq ft. This is still a very low loading compared to 'conventional' aircraft, although higher than for any man-powered aircraft built so far, and one which requires a comparatively large wing area. Since the pilot also has to control the hang-glider on the ground during the take-off and landing, the final machine must not be too large and unwieldy. This points to the need for a wing form embodying large area with low span. In practice this has been achieved in the past with a biplane configuration, and such hang-gliders are still popular today. In addition delta types with sail wings are also used as they comply with the basic requirements of a hang-glider yet can be built more simply.

Figure 3 shows an early design of biplane hang-glider, the construction of which was described in 'Popular Mechanics' published in the United States in April 1909. It was stated that such a gliding machine was a motorless aeroplane, or flying machine, propelled by gravity and designed to carry a passenger through the air from a high point to a lower point some distance away. The construction was to be of spruce and consisted of the following parts.

| | |
|---|---|
| 4 wing spars | ¾in. x 1¼in. x 20 ft. |
| 12 wing cross pieces | ¾in. sq. x 3 ft. |
| 12 wing struts | ½in. x 1½in. x 4ft. |
| 41 wing ribs | 3/16in. x ½in. x 4ft. bent to form the aerofoil shape. |
| 2 arm sticks | 1 in. x 2 in. x 2 ft. |
| 2 rudder sticks | ¾in. sq. x 8 ft. |

together with several pieces ½in. x ¾in. for making the fin and tail plane. The structure was to be braced with no. 16 piano

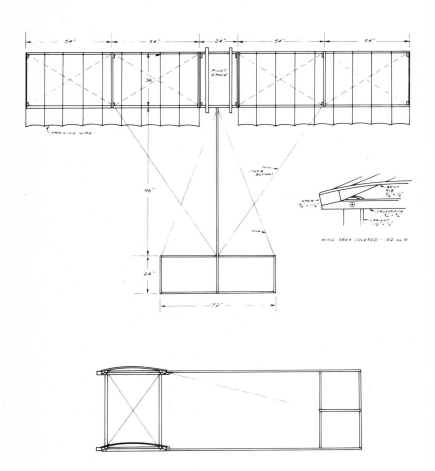

*Figure 3.* 1909 hang glider design.

wire, the bracing being placed horizontally between the spars and cross pieces of the wing, diagonally between the wings in both the longitudinal and lateral directions and from the wings back to the tail surfaces. It was suggested that a suitable covering material for the wings and tail surfaces would be cambric or bleached muslin, the wings being covered on the top surfaces only with an opening in the lower wing for the body of the pilot.

Since the design was evolved in 1909, many improvements, particularly with regard to constructional materials, could be made with today's knowledge. The difficulty of obtaining spruce at the present time could well necessitate a change of the load-carrying structure. For those with some slight engineering skill aluminium alloy tubing can be used instead of spruce and provide a stronger and lighter structure. There are many suitable covering materials such as nylon, although this needs to be doped to make it taut which adds to the cost and the weight. Ordinary polythene sheeting of about 10 thou. thickness is also suitable provided that it is stretched on tightly on a hot day. One of the best coverings is Melinex, an I.C.I. plastic sheeting that is light in weight and can be shrunk after covering by passing a warm iron lightly over it. This type of covering has been used successfully on man-powered aircraft.

The aerodynamic design of the biplane hang-glider shown in Figure 2 is quite adequate for short near-the-ground hops as originally envisaged. When flying such a machine the pilot was instructed to take the glider to the top of a hill, get between the arm sticks and lift the machine, run into the wind for a few steps and leap from the ground. If the air speed and pilot position were correct the glider would continue in free flight down the hill-side. To land the pilot was instructed to push the weight of his body backwards and the glider would then assume a nose-up attitude, slacken speed and settle down to allow the pilot to land safely and gently on his feet. It was further suggested that the beginner should learn by taking short jumps and gradually increase distances as he gained skill in balancing and landing.

This advice is still as relevant today for anyone about to start hang-gliding as it was when first issued, especially a comment to the effect that great care must be exercised on landing otherwise the pilot might suffer a sprained ankle or even a broken limb. Anyone thinking of flying this aircraft or one similar would be well advised to limit flight attempts to wind speeds higher than 15 m.p.h. so that the relative ground speed is low.

Jack Lambie, who has designed a biplane hang-glider similar to that described above, has launched this glider, which he named 'Hang Loose', with the help of three handlers on the ground. Two of the handlers hold the wing tips whilst the third holds the tail unit. All have to release the aircraft together otherwise a ground loop results, but the most critical function is that of the tail man because if he pushes the tail up the glider dives into the ground whilst if he pushes the tail down a stall results. What was apparently required was a gentle level release. Even with expert help from the handlers a stall can result from taking off too slowly. A stall in the air is accompanied by one wing dropping and it is impossible to correct this by weight shifting alone. Also on the flying side Jack Lambie has been tow-launched, the tow being provided by two or more helpers running along the ground with the lines. Obviously the lines should be short, as one very practical rule for hang-gliding is never to go higher than one is prepared to fall, at least during the initial stages of flying. This is such an excellent rule that it should be retained for all hang-glider flying, but human nature being what it is man must go even higher and further.

On the constructional side two improvements to the 1909 design come from Lambie's experience. One is the use of thicker tail booms, and the other the effective sealing of the centre section of the wings. Apparently tail booms increased in thickness to 1in. x 2in. help during ground loops. With regard to the wings, leaks in the upper wings and behind the pilot reduce the overall lift and by disturbing the flow increase the drag, so that these areas should be effectively sealed.

Biplane hang-gliders continued in quite widespread use until the mid 1920's when the Germans began to develop high performance gliders for extended soaring flights. It is interesting to note that Franz Villinger, who worked on the pre-war 'Mufli' man-powered aircraft, entered aviation through hang-gliding. Whilst studying mechanical engineering at the Technical University in Karlsruhr he was a founder member of the local gliding club and started flying in 1927 by air-hopping with a Pelzner hang-glider.

A *Pelzner* hang glider being flown by Franz Villinger of *Mufli* fame, 1927. *Franz Villinger*

Hang-gliders were insufficiently controllable at the time for slope soaring and quite unsuitable for flying in thermals. On the constructional side pilot protection and comfort were important considerations for long flights at relatively high altitudes. Furthermore during the mid 1920's design knowledge regarding low speed aerodynamics had progressed to the stage where conventional gliders were far more sohpis-ticated than hang-gliders, and this position has been retained ever since in terms of pure performance.

The usual simple criteria for judging the performance of gliders is the lift to drag ratio (L/D). Without going into great detail the duration of a glider flight depends on the glide angle and it can be shown quite easily that this is equal to its L/D ratio. Gliders of all types work by flying continuously in a dive so that the influence of gravity can be used to overcome the drag. If the glider flies into a rising airstream that is moving upwards faster than the glider is sinking then it will climb, although still being in a dive, and it is by this means that the duration and distance of glider flights can be ex-tended. Such up-currents are provided by the wind blowing up the sides of hills for slope soaring, or by thermals. How-ever, up-currents are not continuous and as soon as a glider pilot has gained maximum altitude he has to leave if he wishes to fly across country in the hope of finding another thermal before being forced to land. All things being equal, the longer he can fly the better his chance of finding another thermal and this depends on the glide angle and therefore on the L/D ratio of the glider. What is equally important is that with a smaller glide angle the lower will be the rate of sink and the more effectively can the glider gain altitude within an up-current.

This is a basic and somewhat idealistic view of the problem but it gives an idea of how important the L/D ratio is in a glider. Actually today's high performance sailplanes have wing flaps in order to provide a good speed range over which a high L/D ratio is effective so that maximum height can be gained in thermals but the flying time between thermals reduced to a minimum. A more detailed discussion of soaring flight is outside the scope of this book but interested readers are referred to the book 'New Soaring Pilot'.

A glider with a L/D ratio of 30 will be able to fly twice as far as one with an equivalent ratio of 15 in still air conditions.

Because a hang-glider has the pilot hanging in the air stream its aerodynamics are anything but ideal. The drag of hang-gliders is far greater than that of equivalent gliders with enclosed cockpits, the best L/D ratio achieved with a hang-glider is probably of the order of 10 whilst present day sailplanes have ratios of between 40 and 50. On this basis alone it is probable that hang-gliding would have died a natural death after the 1920's except among the few exponents who always surround such activities, if it had not been for the Second World War and the development of the Rogallo parawing. Dealing with these in chronological order, flying for fun was forbidden in the United States during the war within a distance of 150 miles from the coast. This inspired Volmer Jensen to build a hang-glider as he reasoned that as he only intended sliding down a hill-side this could not be confused with flying. Having had some previous experience with hang-gliders he decided that control by weight shifting was inadequate and that full controls were necessary.

The resulting glider, the Volmer VJ-11, was started in 1940 and completed in six weeks of spare time. Full controls were

*Volmer VJ-11* controllable biplane hang glider, 1940. *Derek Morgan*

incorporated, the elevator and ailerons being controlled by the right hand with a cross bar and the rudder by the left hand with a short rudder bar. These controls are also of interest in man-powered flight as the pilot has a similar problem of controlling the aircraft without being able to use the legs on the rudder bar in the conventional manner. Apparently the Volmer hang-glider is very easy to fly especially for anyone who has had previous glider experience, as it has been flown not only by the designer but by many other pilots without any mishap. Jensen suggests that hang-gliding is a very exhilarating branch of aviation and, as long as controls are used, a very safe sport. He goes on to say that as soon as one's feet leave the ground by 12 inches one feels as though one is flying 1000 feet up in the air.

The Volmer fully controlled biplane hang-glider is still being flown today and a complete set of plans can be bought for the home constructor. Cost of materials for this machine will vary with our inflationary economic trends but were quoted by the designer in 1973 as being of the order of £50. Jensen has continued with hang glider development due to the wide spread interest in this subject and has created a new monoplane design called 'Swingwing', nothing to do with the swingwing concept of Barnes Wallis that was incorporated in the American F-111 bomber, but a fixed monoplane configuration that is described later. Volmer's 'Swingwing' is of interest as it provides an improvement in performance on previous hang-glider designs. Meanwhile the controllable hang-glider does seem to have many advantages for the beginner in the field although it tends to conflict with the basic merits of the hang-glider, namely cheapness and simplicity. Perhaps in the future some compromise solution can be evolved with a hang-glider designed with inherent stability.

Completing this brief review of biplane hang-gliders is a tailless swept wing aircraft that first flew in 1971. This glider, built by Taras Kiceniuk, was appropriately named 'Icarus'. Figure 4 shows the configuration of this design which in-

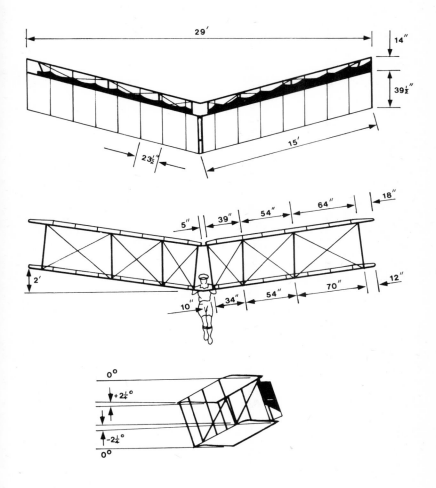

*Figure 4. Icarus* hang glider.

corporates a rudder control but relied on weight shifting for lateral and longitudinal control. With the combination of dihedral and sweep back angles, stability should be good and this has been borne out by the excellent flights achieved in practice. In October 1971, Taras Kiceniuk Jr. made several flights above the beach at Torrance, California, during which he made one slope soaring flight of 5 minutes. This was a particularly successful flight as most hang-glider enthusiasts still tend to measure performance in terms of seconds rather than minutes and especially as in this case a total gain in height of some 70 feet above the take-off point was also achieved. Many hang-gliders had previously recorded longer flights but only as a result of a loss of altitude. Since then, of course, hang-glider endurance records have been extended until they are now measured in hours. At the same site at Torrance a record flight was made in July 1973 with a different form of hang-glider, a delta sail wing configuration of the Rogallo type described later, that lasted for 3 hours 36 minutes. This is not quoted as a record, as it has already been beaten, but as a measure of the development in hang-gliding from 1971 to 1973. One notices these jumps in performance attainment during particular periods with most sports and this indicates that hang-gliding is simply following the pattern. Record flights for hang-gliders are no longer restricted by aerodynamic considerations but by the more practical ones of pilot comfort and the limitation to the hours of daylight.

The 'Icarus' hang-glider obviously had a good L/D ratio to give such an excellent performance and this must have been due in part to the elimination of tail surfaces, which reduced both the drag and the weight of the machine; also to the fact that for that particular flight Taras was sitting under the glider in a nylon seat belt. Only by using such a support can one fly for any length of time without becoming exhausted and the use of such a seat reduces the frontal area of the pilot with a noticeable decrease in the overall drag of the hang-glider. However before being able to use such a seat the pilot must first become proficient in controlling the hang-glider in the 'normal' position.

Apparently the particular flight with 'Icarus' mentioned above was deliberately curtailed, so clearly this type of glider has a great potential and provides encouragement for the development of hang-glider designs. In particular the control system was shown to be successful as the flight of 5 minutes included three 180° turns all made using rudder control alone. The 'Icarus' rudders tended to function more as drag plates than as conventional rudders. Such a control system is again of direct interest to man-powered aircraft designers.

Other models have been developed including a monoplane flying wing form, but the majority of hang-glider enthusiasts still use simple machines that can more readily be built by the home constructor and are based on the Rogallo parawing. Although not the only type of sail wing, the Rogallo is the simplest and is sufficiently stable to be flown without the need of additional control surfaces. Based on a patent by Francis Rogallo for a kite design shown in Figure 5, the

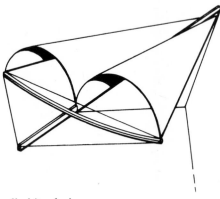

*Figure 5. Rogallo* kite design.

parawing has found application in several areas of aviation. Although strictly a flexible lifting surface, the parawing has also been called the paraglider, flex-wing, flexkite or flight sail. Apart from its application for kites and hang-gliders it has been used as a rocket booster recovery glider, a powered flex-wing built by the Ryan Aircraft Company, a Fleep or flying jeep, cargo paraglider and an unmanned cargo-tow glider.

These applications indicate not only the flexibility of the wing construction but also its usefulness to aviation. The Rogallo parawing has been thoroughly tested in the wind tunnel. Static and dynamic lateral and longitudinal stability have been shown to be good at moderate angles of attack. At too high an angle the glider generally experiences a fugoid oscillation which causes an up and down snaking motion, whilst at too low an angle the canopy luffs at the untethered trailing edge which creates a very unstable condition. The best angle of attack is of the order of 20° at which it provides a lift coefficient $(C_L)$ of about 0.6, this being a measure of the lifting characteristics of the wing section. To put this value in perspective it may be stated that a typical value for $C_L$ is 1 for most low speed aircraft applications.

Overall L/D ratio for the Rogallo wing is of the order of 7 at the 20° angle of attack, although this value can vary with aspect ratio according to the comparative sizes of the wing span and chord. Figure 6 shows the variation of L/D ratio with lift coefficient for two aspect ratio wings of 3 and 6 respectively. Designing with a lower aspect ratio ensures a greater wing area for a given span and this in turn means a lower flying speed which is generally more suitable for hang-gliding applications. Some high aspect ratio Rogallo hang-gliders have been built in order to extend performance by increasing the L/D ratio, thereby improving the glide angle. However slots, auxiliary aerofoils and special control surfaces are required to make such gliders workable.

Richard Miller, at one time editor of 'Soaring', the American

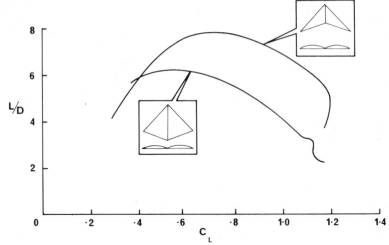

*Figure 6. Rogallo* parawing performance.

magazine on gliding, was one of the first to realise the potential application of the Rogallo parawing to hang-gliding. He built such an aircraft using bamboo for the primary structure and Mylar plastic sheet, the American equivalent of Melinex, for the sail. Appropriately called the 'Bamboo Butterfly', this aircraft first flew in January 1966. The pilot was suspended from a set of parallel supports which he also held to maintain control. Miller indicates that there are two approaches to controlling such a glider, either by moving the aircraft about with relation to the pilot's mass or by weight shifting underneath the glider. With the former method the pilot has a control bar which he can move with relation to his body in order to exercise control, with the latter he can be imagined to be freely supported under the aircraft and can move his body about for control. It is easier to think of the first approach whilst the pilot's feet are still on the ground, and the latter approach whilst in the air.

Miller's first flights took place from a slope facing into wind. The take-off run started about ten feet from the crest of the hill and continued some six or seven feet down the slope. Against an 8 to 10 knot wind with 150 sq. ft. of sail area he found difficulty in running unless the sail angle were set for minimum drag. This angle proved to be less than the normal angle of attack for flight and one at which the sail just began to luff. His technique was to keep the sail on the point of luffing throughout the take-off run, which necessitated a change of angle of the wing when going from the level to the slope. If the angle of attack were too high the drag was too great but if the angle were too low the glider 'nosed' in. The ideal was to keep the glider at the necessary angle during take-off and then rotate the nose up to the correct flying position only when the flying speed had been achieved. In practice it has proved to be easier to take off into a higher wind speed with only a small difference between the wind and flying speeds.

Once in the air Miller found that lateral control required all his gymnastic experience, whilst longitudinal control required only small movements. Miller described the movements for longitudinal control as being 'subtle' and apparently on one flight made three or four longitudinal oscillations simply by small movements of his left foot. Turns with a Rogallo glider are flat skidding arcs with no bank at all, as is to be expected with an aircraft having no lateral controls. Landings are generally supposed to be easy, fortunately as the pilot cannot put this manœuvre off until a more favourable opportunity, it simply being a case of rotating the sail or the pilot swinging his legs backwards until the glider slows down and allows the pilot to run in to a landing. The main problem is to prevent the glider stalling on landing although some help could be expected from a Rogallo sail wing acting as a parachute. Since these early experiences by Miller, Rogallo hang-glider design has developed to the extent that flying is made easier and some pilots claim it to be second nature once airborne.

Flights can be extended once experience has been gained by short hops. One of the main dangers when flying at higher altitudes is of stalling in turning flight. The other main danger when flying Rogallo gliders is of the sail luffing whilst in a dive and the pilot losing longitudinal control because of it. There were five deaths in the United States alone in 1973 amongst hang-glider enthusiasts that can be attributed solely to this.

It is suggested that a stalling situation developed during a turn killed the pioneer Lilienthal and still provides a danger to hang-gliders today. Stalling during turns results from the difficulty of estimating the airspeed and maintaining it, aggravated by the low wing loadings of hang-gliders. With regard to the airspeed, one problem is the difficulty of gaining sufficient experience due to the shortness of most flights; another is the lack of any reference source on the glider to help the pilot to estimate his flying speed. There is also a tendency to pull up in turning flight in order to get away from the ground and to gain more altitude to prevent scraping a wing tip, which further reduces the airspeed. Low wing loadings are satisfactory in level flight but in turning there is a possibility that the differential in wing-tip flying speeds will cause the inner wing tip to stall.

Richard Miller has suggested an audible airspeed indicator as one possible solution to this problem. For this application he has checked out the use of a pitch pipe as used for tuning musical instruments. With a pitch pipe used for tuning a Cello, the instrument having four pipes, the low note started sounding at about 16 m.p.h. and increased in volume until reaching a peak at about 25 m.p.h. Throughout the range no change in pitch was noticed. The higher notes came in at higher speeds so that a full range of speeds could be measured by using different notes on a particular pitch pipe or by using different pipes. Miller has also tested such a pitch pipe at various angles to the air flow and found that there was no noticeable change up to angles of 20° to 25°.

Although hang-gliding is dangerous when practiced at high altitude, and unfortunately this point must be stressed especially as the pilot's body is unprotected in the event of a crash, it is becoming increasingly more popular as a sport. Many people fly Rogallo hang-gliders because of their basic simplicity. They were portrayed in the early 1970's as being the cheapest and simplest of aircraft and it was said they could be built in less than 100 man-hours for less than £100.

On finding the limitations of the 'Bamboo Butterfly'

The *Conduit Condor*, an aluminium structure covered with a Mylar plastic transparent surface, flown by Richard Millar in the late '60s. *Derek Morgan*

Miller built a more sophisticated Rogallo based on an aluminium tubular structure, appropriately named the 'Conduit Condor'. This had a jib sail over the leading edge, which in aeronautical jargon is usually described as an auxiliary aerofoil, which greatly improved the basic performance of the simple Rogallo parawing. Many such developments have been made in order to improve the performance of Rogallo gliders, but they tend to detract from the inherent simplicity of the Rogallo wing form which is the main reason for its popularity.

Figure 7 illustrates a typical Rogallo hang-glider configuration. This typical design is similar to that used by Dave Kilbourne, who is one of the pioneers in the use of Rogallo gliders and is a very experienced hang-glider pilot in the United States, the glider having a 16 feet keel with a 40° wing angle and an angle of 44° on the sail cloth which was of 4 oz. dacron. In order to allow the pilot to operate in comfort for long flights he is supported by a seat, the plastic type used for a child's swing, which was held out of the way by a car seat belt during the initial take-off run. Apparently the control by weight shifting with this type of Rogallo glider

*Figure 7.* Typical *Rogallo* hang glider configuration.

is very sensitive. It has a minimum speed of about 10 m.p.h. with the stall coming in gently, whilst the maximum speed was about 35 m.p.h. This maximum speed is too great for most hang-glider applications because of the unprotected pilot position in the event of a crash. Although this order of speed is low by normal aeronautical standards the unprotected pilot crashing into an obstacle at 35 m.p.h. is in the same position as someone falling from a height of 40 feet, with the same inevitable results. Several deaths of hang-glider enthusiasts have been noted due to this very problem of pilots colliding with obstacles either on or near the ground during high speed flight. No one would fall from a height of 40 feet on purpose, so no pilot should venture to a position in which a high speed collision is even remotely possible. A collision at a more reasonable speed of 20 m.p.h. is equivalent to a fall of only 13 feet, which although bad enough would probably not have quite the same catastrophic results. A low

An early *Eipper 'Flexi-flier'* low aspect ratio Rogallo with a vinyl sail. A 'kite' like this is relatively inexpensive but is not very suitable for ambitious flights. *John McMasters*

*Volmer Jensen 'Sunfun'*, a sophisticated hang glider with good gliding properties, developed from the VJ 23. *John McMasters.*

speed landing is certainly indicated because by comparison a 10 m.p.h. collision is equivalent to a fall of only 3½ feet.

Dace Kilbourne has made some thousand flights with Rogallo hang-gliders, the highest being at 2,500 feet above ground level and the longest being 25 minutes of ridge soaring. With a glide angle of only 5 to 1 this latter performance was quite an achievement and is an indication of his expertise in this field, an expertise that was gained through much practice. Before even attempting to fly over land he made hundreds of towed hops behind a speedboat over water. In this way his flying speed was controlled by the boat and he could practise his piloting and also test his glider whilst having a relatively soft landing when things did not behave quite as planned.

One of the most sophisticated hang-gliders built so far is the Volmer 'Swingwing VJ-23' fully controlled monoplane built in 1973. Technically it had an excellent performance for a hang-glider having a L/D ratio of 9 with the pilot in a hanging position. Wingspan was nearly 33 feet with a wing area of 179 sq. ft. and a flying weight of 300 lb. This weight included 200 lb of Volmer Jensen. With a cruising flying speed of 20 m.p.h. and a stalling speed of 15 m.p.h., the Swingwing was capable of self soaring flight in reasonably high wind speeds. According to Volmer Jensen it was possible to take-off in a 15 m.p.h. breeze and gain altitude immediately. Even using a hill only 35 feet high with a 20° to 25° slope it has been possible to climb.

Construction of the wing incorporated a leading edge of 1/32 inch poplar plywood and the remainder was covered with lightweight aircraft fabric doped sufficiently to be non-porous. Wheels were incorporated to facilitate movement on the ground but could be removed for flight. Usually they were retained during flight so as to take some of the shocks of a mis-timed landing.

It has been suggested that an improvement in the performance of hang-gliders can be obtained through the use of man power to extend the glide. However, even if a workable propulsion system can be devised there is still the problem of controlling the glider whilst also powering it. It is also questionable whether using man power is worth it in terms of the performance improvement. If we consider a typical hang-glider with a weight of say 200 lb. in flying trim with a glide angle of 1 in 5, i.e. a L/D ratio of 5, this means that the total drag in flight is of the order of 40 lb. A pilot working hard could probably provide a propulsive thrust of about 8 lb. so that the new glide angle with the use of man power could be improved to about 1 in 6½. Such an improvement would be worth while if it meant getting from a region of poor lift for extended soaring but is of debatable value for non-soaring flights.

One method of powering a hang-glider that has been tentatively suggested is by means of 'pseudo-ornithopter' propulsion. Pseudo-ornithopter because instead of the wings moving up and down, the pilot moves up and down. The argument goes, and has been backed by a mathematical analysis of the problem, that if in flight the pilot is crouching on a platform under the wing and then suddenly stands up he is imparting energy to the aircraft. This will cause the aircraft to rise and at the same time the pilot can lower his body again to a crouching position, trying to keep the centre of gravity of the aircraft in a constant position whilst doing so. Then the pilot can suddenly stand up again.

In theory this mode of propulsion has possibilities and it is argued further that children use a similar form of propulsion whilst swinging. However in practice the energy may not go into the system as useful work at all but could show up as extra drag because of the movements of the pilot and the up-and-down motion of the glider. The basic argument has been propounded on the basis of the glider being rigid, which is difficult to relate to a typical hang-glider and is certainly not the case with the Rogallo parawing.

Hang-glider flying is now highly developed particularly in the United States, where they have their own organisation — Self-Soar Association Inc. Based at Santa Monica, California, this organisation co-ordinates activities and also publishes a journal 'Low and Slow' to record and publicise new developments in hang-gliding. Several competitions have been held as being the only suitable form of activity for measuring, as well as providing an inspiration for, improvements in hang-gliding.

Following these developments in the United States the hang-glider movement has spread round the world and has many enthusiasts in Europe and Australia. The simplicity of the sport has particular appeal in the highly developed countries. One of the most notable hang-glider achievements in Britain was a flight in the Autumn of 1973 by Kenneth Messenger from Snowdon, a mountain in North Wales. Using a Rogallo glider weighing 33 lb. he was transported to the top by means of the Snowdon rack-and-pinion mountain railway, then launched from near the summit and after a 15 minute flight landed in the Nant Gwynant valley at the foot of the mountains.

A British competition which, although aimed at general man-powered flight, has attracted some interest from hang-glider enthusiasts is the Selsey International Bird-Man Rally. Originally started by Patrick Moore the astronomer, this rally is now organised by the local branch of the Royal Air Forces Association at Selsey, a town in Sussex that is situated on the south coast of England. Originally £500, the prize has now been increased to £3000 for the first flight of 50 yards when launched from a 30 feet high pier.

The basic rules for the competition are that home-made wings of not more than 30 feet span may be used together with any form of flapping or propeller man power drive. Take-off must be from the pier under the pilot's own power and a distance of 4 yards is available for the take-off run. The flights are made over the sea, so the competitors must satisfy the judges that they can swim and that if the wings are attached to the pilot's body a quick release device is incorporated. A further safety requirement is that the competitor must wear a life jacket. Each competitor is allowed two flight attempts.

Such a rally obviously attracts the extreme type of competitor, the bird-man who straps wings to his arms and then launches himself flailing his arms madly and creates a big splash and perhaps a bigger launch. It has also attracted some serious attempts and the best flight up till now has been with a Rogallo hang-glider. Although short of the necessary 50 yards this flight gave promise of further hang-glider participation.

The basic glide angle of 1 in 5 for this course is within the capabilities of hang-gliders, but this is only relevant in still air conditions. The speed of the craft with relation to the air is the sum of both the take-off speed and the wind speed. As the glider relies more on wind speed to ensure flight, the effective glide ratio also has to increase. For example if the flying speed was 10 m.p.h. and this was made up of a take-off speed of 5 m.p.h. and a wind speed of 5 m.p.h. the effective glide angle to achieve the course would be 1 in 10. Although the aircraft would be flying at 10 m.p.h. it is still only covering the ground at 5 m.p.h. So the major problem is of accelerating to the necessary flying speed within the 4 yards available on the pier.

There seems to be little point in including any man-powered system within the aircraft designed for such a rally, as indeed there is little point in including such propulsion systems within hang-gliders in general, since only a small improvement in performance could be expected for a considerably increased complexity of construction and operation. It would appear most sensible within these low-speed branches of aviation that man-power systems be retained for use solely within true man-powered aircraft.

# 3

# Man-powered aircraft

This chapter in no way sets out to present a history of man-powered aircraft, nor is it possible to discuss all man-powered aircraft that have been built. The purpose is to describe fifteen aircraft that have been built during the post-war era and that have actually flown. Each of the aircraft represents a stage in the development of man-powered flight and can provide a guide for future achievements. Details of the fifteen man-powered aircraft that have flown are listed below in Table 1:—

Table 1.

| | Span (ft.) | Wing Area (ft.$^2$) | Aspect Ratio | Empty Weight (lb.) | Flying Weight (lb.) | Wing Loading (lb./ft.$^2$) | Country | First Flight |
|---|---|---|---|---|---|---|---|---|
| SUMPAC | 80 | 300 | 21.3 | 128 | 269 | 0.90 | U K. | 1961 |
| Puffin 1 | 84 | 330 | 21.4 | 118 | 267 | 0.81 | U.K. | 1961 |
| Puffin II | 93 | 390 | 22.0 | 140 | 290 | 0.78 | U.K. | 1965 |

| | Span (ft.) | Wing Area (ft.²) | Aspect Ratio | Empty Weight | Flying Weight | Wing Loading | Country | First Flight |
|---|---|---|---|---|---|---|---|---|
| Reluctant Phoenix | 33 | 250 | 4.4 | 38 | 180 | 0.71 | U.K. | 1965 |
| Linnet I | 73 | 288 | 18.5 | 105 | 230 | 0.80 | Japan | 1965 |
| Linnet II | 73 | 280 | 19 | 99 | 225 | 0.80 | Japan | 1967 |
| Linnet III | 83 | 325 | 21.2 | 111 | 232 | 0.72 | Japan | 1970 |
| Linnet IV | 83 | 336 | 21.9 | 119 | 237 | 0.75 | Japan | 1971 |
| Malliga Aircraft | 64 | 262 | 15.6 | 113 | 239 | 0.91 | Austria | 1967 |
| Dumbo | 120 | 480 | 30.0 | 125 | 276 | 0.57 | U.K. | 1971 |
| Jupiter | 79 | 308 | 20.1 | 146 | 296 | 0.96 | U.K. | 1972 |
| Wright Aircraft | 71 | 480 | 10.5 | 90 | 240 | 0.50 | U.K. | 1972 |
| Liverpuffin | 64 | 305 | 13.4 | 140 | 300 | 0.99 | U.K. | 1972 |
| Toucan | 123 | 600 | 25.0 | 209 | 519 | 0.85 | U.K. | 1972 |
| Hurel Aviette | 132 | 581 | 30.0 | 145 | 295 | 0.51 | France | 1974 |

By excluding many man-powered aircraft projects from the list in Table 1 it may be argued that it is not complete or sufficiently representative to be of value in a book of this nature. However one's criterion must always be, 'does it work?', and the list in Table 1 has been chosen because the aircraft listed do work. Anybody can have a good idea, the world abounds in thinkers rather than doers and nowhere is this more apparent than in man-powered flight, but for good ideas to be accepted they must be proved in practice. It is hoped that this emphasis on the practical aspects of man-powered flight will not inhibit innovation but rather persuade people to have the courage of their convictions and prove their ideas in practice.

The man-powered aircraft described in Table 1 will be briefly discussed in the order listed as, although this is not strictly chronological, the development behind each aircraft will be dealt with in chronological order. For example the Linnet IV was built and flown after the Malliga aircraft but the development behind Linnet IV started much earlier with Linnet I. Development of all the aircraft listed can be directly related to the Kremer prizes, although in the case of Liverpuffin the link is rather tenuous. Both of the earlier aircraft were built as a direct result of the first offer of the £5,000 Kremer prize in 1957 and with the financial support of the Man-Powered Aircraft Group of the Royal Aeronautical Society.

## SUMPAC

The Southampton University Man-Powered Aircraft, SUMPAC for short, was built by three post-graduate students — David Williams, Anne Marsden and Alan Lassiere. The idea of building a man-powered aircraft came to them during lectures in their undergraduate course early in 1960, but the design work did not start in earnest until after their final examinations in the following July. Construction started in early 1961 and after the Royal Aeronautical Society awarded the group £1,500 in February, 1961, work progressed rapidly so that the machine was completed by September, 1961.

Design started with the pilot as there was little information to work on, and power tests were performed on members of a local cycling club. Eventually it was decided to have the pilot in a reclining position as this would minimise the frontal area of the aircraft and thereby reduce drag, taking the leg thrust on the back and leaving the arms free to manipulate the controls. Furthermore it provided a satisfactory power output whilst also being comfortable. In this the Southampton group came to conclusions similar to those of Haessler and Villinger in the 1930's who chose a fully reclining position for their 'Mufli' aircraft. A single-seater arrangement was chosen as being the simplest, there being no real, technical advantages in two-seater or multi-seater aircraft. This set the fashion for most man-powered aircraft projects as all those listed in Table 1, apart from Toucan, are single-seater machines.

As the Southampton group were really working in the dark regarding man-powered flight, since there was no previous experience to base their design on, they sensibly chose a conventional configuration and used well-tried conventional materials such as wood and fabric for the construction. Thought was given to 'modern' materials such as plastics but it was decided not to use them on the basis of the extra time required to devise new techniques to use their properties efficiently. Once the aircraft had been designed a 1/16 scale model was tested in the wind tunnel to check on the drag, lift and pitching behaviour in flight. It was found that, following some small modifications to improve the air flow at the pylon/wing junction, the measured values agreed very closely with those already calculated.

For ease of travelling and handling on the ground the wing was made in three sections. To simplify problems of jigging during construction and to counteract aerodynamic twisting, the wing primary structure was based on two spars. The spars were made of laminated spruce with girder webs between in the vertical direction and joined by horizontal cross bracing to form a stiff torsion box and therefore a wing sufficiently stiff to withstand twisting. Ribs were used to provide the aerofoil shape and these were of girder form made of spruce and balsa wood. Conventional ailerons were constructed integral with the wing to eliminate a separate jig and were detached later. All the necessary metal fittings were bonded to the wood by means of Araldite epoxy resin thereby eliminating bolts and so saving weight. Wood joints were made using Cascamite ureaformaldehyde synthetic resin. Wing covering was by doped nylon, this being chosen for its lightness and strength. Originally two coats of ordinary glider dope were used to tighten the nylon giving a weight of 2 oz/ sq. yard, but because of the slackening effect of the damp atmosphere at the airfield a further two coats had to be applied. This increased the final weight to some 6 lb. above the estimated weight, indicating the need for realistic initial assumptions and careful weight control during construction.

All the main loads were taken on a lightweight aluminium structure to which the wings and fuselage were bolted. The drive mechanism consisted of a 3/32" Renold chain to drive the 27" racing cycle drive wheel from the pedals. It was decided to gear the propeller to the drive wheel permanently by a twisted flat steel belt coated with 'belt-stick' to prevent slipping. This decision to gear the wheel and propeller together was based on the assumption that the wheel would be free to rotate during flight and although this might affect the power output of the pilot a little it would minimise possible shock loadings on landing. Again this decision by the Southampton group has been used on all other man-powered aircraft that have driven undercarriages. The propeller was constructed of solid balsa sandwiched between plywood ribs supported by a main structure of an aluminium tube. Here the group were again working in an unknown area, that of designing a suitable propeller of very high efficiency for the low power input of the pilot. They were fortunate in being able to check their actual propeller in the wind tunnel under full scale conditions, the propeller being designed to rotate at 240 rpm, at a flying speed of 30 ft./sec.

SUMPAC was flown at Lasham airfield with Derek Piggott as the pilot. It had originally been decided that members of the group would learn to fly gliders so that they could handle the man-powered aircraft. In view of the anticipated difficulty of control and the time and money invested in its construction the decision to use an expert pilot of Derek Piggott's calibre was probably the wisest one. At the time of the first flight he described the machine as quite a 'handful' and that flying it was outside the ability of the average pilot. More recently he wrote:

"Few people know what the Southampton students went

The *SUMPAC* in flight at Lasham airfield in 1962, piloted by Derek Piggott. *Author's collection*

through during their attempts. Because we had no hangarage available most of the time (3 - 4 months) we had to rig and de-rig each day. It took three hours to rig after the 25 miles' drive to the flying field. The building in which it was stored was so leaky that the aircraft was very wet on almost every flying day. Usually by the time it was rigged the wind had sprung up and on the day of arrival after lunch the aircraft was flown at dusk with dew on the fabric."

It is difficult to overpraise the achievements of the Southampton group because at each stage they were working under difficult conditions against a background of uncertainty as to whether their project would actually succeed. A problem that came to light during the first taxi-ing trials was the difficulty of using the unconventional controls, the aircraft being entirely controlled by a stick, rather than stick and rudder as with normal aircraft. Also the undercarriage had to be modified. The support frame had to be strengthened, and the front wheel simplified to a 9" solid wheel that was free to caster.

The second series of taxi-ing attempts were made on a rough runway, the extra drag of the rough surface limiting speeds to the calculated minimum required to fly. Wheel slipping occurred which indicated that the machine was just airborne, but at this stage a serious swing developed. On the

9th November, 1961, after the familiar routine of swinging off the runway several times, Derek Piggott made a determined effort to keep accelerating after the weight came off the wheel and slipping began. Quite suddenly he found the aircraft climbing in a rather nose high attitude whereupon he overcontrolled with the elevator and dived back to earth. By the third attempt he was more familiar with the controls and had a longer and smoother flight of 50 yards including a climb under power to 5 ft. above the runway.

Study of cine films made of the first flights showed the aircraft to be in a semi-stalled condition and the propeller gearing was then changed to provide more thrust at higher flying speeds. Next attempts were made on the 24th-25th November, and required much less effort, one of the flights lasting for 30 seconds, which was equivalent to 300 yards' length under still air conditions. Altogether some 40 flights were made with SUMPAC including 80° turns and a maximum flight length of 650 yards in late 1962.

In 1964 a group at Imperial College, London, under the leadership of Alan Lassiere, who was one of the original members of the Southampton group, took the aircraft over and did a partial re-design. This consisted largely of an improved drive system with the original steel belt being replaced by a positive drive belt. The aircraft was damaged when, with a cyclist at the controls, a gust took it to a height of 30 ft. and it then stalled and hit the ground. It has not been flown since but was partially repaired and is now on permanent display at the Shuttleworth Collection, Old Warden Aerodrome, Bedfordshire.

## Puffin I and Puffin II

Puffin I and Puffin II were built by a man-powered aircraft group at Hatfield, many of the members coming from the de Havilland Aircraft Company, including the chairman of the group, John Wimpenny, who was assistant Chief Aerodynamicist, later to become Chief Aerodynamicist of the company. Puffin I first flew on the 16th November, 1961, some few days after SUMPAC, with J. H. Philips, a de Havilland test pilot, at the controls. The configuration of Puffin I was completely different from that of the Southampton machine as the pilot was mounted at the nose in a cycling position. Propeller drive was at the tail just behind the rudder and tailplane in order to minimise drag by not having any part of the aircraft structure within the propeller slip-stream.

As much care and attention went into the design and construction of Puffin as if it were a full-size aircraft project, this approach to the problem stemming from the group's direct contact with the aircraft industry. This approach was also possible because of the large number of people involved in the group's activities. The Royal Aeronautical Society awarded £1,500 towards construction, much of which went on labour, and help was received from the apprentices' school at de Havillands. Also through association with the aircraft industry help was received from other companies; the drive wheel and gearbox were produced by Dunlop, and the propeller was designed and constructed by the Propeller division of de Havillands.

Construction of Puffin I owed much to full size aircraft practice, as the loads were carried by a stressed skin of balsa. In other words the aircraft was sheeted with thin balsa over

*Puffin 1* in flight at de Havilland's airfield at Hatfield. *Hatfield Group*

63

the whole of the fuselage and the leading edge of the wing and the main loads were carried by this sheeting. A supporting internal structure of strip balsa wood was used to preserve the correct shape and prevent distortion under loading. In principle this was-the ideal form of construction with the materials then available, but in practice the balsa sheets tended to warp with changes of temperature and humidity. At times the balsa dried out so much that the whole wing had to be steamed with a kettle in order to increase the moisture level again. Apparently it had also the unnerving habit of creaking and groaning whilst in flight. Owing to the warping of the wing structure ¼ inch thick strips of foam were attached transversely to the surface and the covering attached to the foam strips. This ensured a smooth covering although the final wing profile was a little different from that originally designed. Also the weight of the wing went up during construction, the original weight being estimated at 40 lb. whereas the final weight for Puffin I's wing came to 65 lb.

Performance of Puffin I was good, and for a decade, '62 to '72, it held the record for the longest flight of a man-powered aircraft from a man-powered take-off. This flight was made in May, 1962, with John Wimpenny at the controls, a distance of 993 yards being recorded from unstick to landing. As a result of this the Royal Aeronautical Society awarded a special prize of £50 to the group for the first flight over half a mile. After successfully completing over 90 flights Puffin I crashed in April, 1963, when it took off into a 4-5 knot wind coming at about 10° to the runway. These conditions were within the limits set by previous experience but the pilot in this case was relatively inexperienced with the machine. After climbing steadily to 10 ft. altitude the aircraft drifted away from its course until it was heading out over the grass at about 25°. The pilot applied full rudder but no bank and as this had no effect, the pilot decided to land on the grass rather than attempt a complex turning manœuvre. From 5 ft. height the aircraft sank rapidly to the ground into a boggy area of soft clay which stopped the machine and thereby initiated the break up due to the violent braking effect.

The opportunity was then taken to re-design and re-build the aircraft as Puffin II. The fuselage, tail surfaces and drive/propulsion system from Puffin I were repaired and retained. A completely redesigned wing was employed using the more conventional spar and rib type of construction, incorporating a new and highly efficient aerofoil section created by Dr. Wortmann of Stuttgart University and with a wing-span increased to 93 ft. It was estimated that this would reduce the power requirements at low altitude from about 0.4 h.p. for Puffin I to 0.3 h.p. for Puffin II and thereby enable the pilot to pedal for a longer time.

Puffin II first flew in August, 1965, and although the man-power requirements were an improvement on those of previous machines the handling was not. Because of the larger wing span it was found to be difficult to control the machine directionally with conventional rudder and ailerons. Wing tip drag brakes therefore had to be added which were interconnected with the rudder controls in order to get the machine to turn. These allowed the aircraft to execute a 270° turn which is the most achieved by any man-powered aircraft to date. In terms of flight lengths Puffin II's performance was not much better than that achieved by Puffin I for various reasons, the most obvious being that as the flying speed was lower the pilot had to pedal for a longer time to achieve the same result. However the main reasons were connected with the handling characteristics because the pilot had to devote more attention to controlling the machine. Also, with such a large aircraft representing so much cost and effort, flying was restricted to calm conditions thereby limiting flying to some 20 flights a year and so limiting the flying experience of the pilots.

Flying Puffin was normally restircted to near dusk in order to get calm conditions but after some 90 flights it

*Puffin II* flying at maximum altitude of nearly 20ft. with John Wimpenny at the controls. *Hatfield Group*

eventually crashed in early 1969. The pilot veered away from a region of turbulent air which was encountered at a height of 6 ft. above the runway during supposedly calm conditions. Whilst executing this manœuvre the aircraft struck a landing light with the result that the fuselage was destroyed together with most of the wing ribs. Faced with this immense rebuilding task the Hatfield group decided that after working for ten years with Puffin they would not continue with the project. The remains were eventually given to Liverpool University and some parts incorporated in Liverpuffin which by its name acknowledges the association with the Puffin.

## Reluctant Phoenix

A few months before Puffin II was flown in 1965 another British man-powered aircraft had also flown — the 'Reluctant Phoenix', which was the last inflatable machine designed and built by Perkins. This machine had a delta wing arrangement with a cut-out in the centre for the pilot. It had two fixed fins on the wing tips for stabilising and a movable propeller /rudder assembly behind the main fin. The most notable features of the aircraft were that, being inflatable, its empty weight was only 38 lb. and it could be dismantled and deflated to fit inside a car boot.

*Reluctant Phoenix*, Dan Perkins' successful inflatable man-powered aircraft, being rigged in the airship hanger at Cardington. *Author's collection*

Learning from his earlier unsuccessful machines, described in Chapter 1, Perkins increased the wing area to 250 sq. ft.

thereby allowing a more realistic wing loading of nearly 0.7lb/sq. ft.

The structure of the aircraft could be considered to be in two parts, the primary structure of the 'fuselage' and the inflatable wing structure. The primary structure consisted of a single aluminium tube running fore and aft the central 'fuselage' section of 2 inch diameter at the forward end and 1 inch at the rear. This tube supported the nose wheel, which incidentally was steerable, pilot, transmission system, controls and the fin post at the rear of the main central fin.

The pilot was seated in a reclining position with pedals and seat at the same level. Drive mechanism consisted of a continuous rope belt drive over pulleys at the pedals, at the base of the fin post and at the propeller drive shaft. To improve contact between belt and pulleys and so reduce slip, the belt was coated with polyurethane which, according to Dan Perkins, is most suitable for this purpose. The propeller was of 8½ ft. diameter and similar to the ones used on the earlier Perkins machines.

Wing construction was of 1 oz./sq. yard nylon covered with polyurethane in order to prevent leakage. Most of the loading was taken by the nylon, as the only additional supports were short bracing wires from the wheels to the wings at points less than 1/5th of the span out from the centre. The shape was maintained and the loads taken by diaphragms hand-stitched in position and then taped over the outside to prevent leakage. Air pressure required to inflate the wings was quite low at 12 inches of water gauge, that is approximately 0.4 p.s.i. Wing weight alone was 13 lb. for a wing of 33 ft. span using an aerofoil section with a thickness to chord ratio of 20%.

Dan Perkins had intended to try to fly 'Reluctant Phoenix' himself but in view of his lack of success with the previous three machines it is perhaps fortunate that he managed to enlist the help of a trained cyclist, Mike Street. In all 96 flights were made with this aircraft, most of them from winch assisted take-offs but with at least four from unassisted take-offs. The take-off run was of the order of 140 yards from which the aircraft climbed to about 2 ft. altitude.

All the flights were made in the 800 ft. long airship hangar at Cardington because there was no outdoor runway available.

Reluctant Phoenix was very nearly the first woman-powered aircraft. Mike Street's wife was also a trained cyclist and some 1½ stone lighter than her husband. However, she was pregnant throughout the course of the flight trials.

Dan Perkins recalls that on one of the earlier flights the aircraft veered to the side of the hangar and struck a balloon cable that punctured the skin, causing it to deflate. They ran to the aircraft to find it all crumpled with a large still bulge in the middle — the pilot. His wife shouted "Mike are you all right?" and as this caused no movement they were panic stricken until eventually a muffled voice answered, "But Mr. Perkins told me that whatever happened I must sit still for fear of damaging the structure!!"

Weight is of the greatest importance with a man-powered aircraft and Dan Perkins recalls that he spent a week, working during the evenings, in developing the aircraft and managed to save 2 lb. Mike Street came along at the weekend having lost 7 lb. without any effort other than going on a week's diet.

After the 96 flights they decided that the Kremer prize was outside the performance capabilities of 'Reluctant Phoenix' and so the project was terminated. At the same time Dan Perkins was blessed with a daughter, by his second wife, so he decided to devote the remainder of his life to her. Having given 6 years of his spare time and holidays to man-powered flight, even spending one cold Boxing Day in a hangar without any form of heating, he decided that he had done enough. It was now up to others!

In retrospect the Perkins 'Reluctant Phoenix' was successful in that it did fly and was probably the most transportable man-powered aircraft ever built.

Because of this it is anticipated that further inflatable man-powered aircraft will be built in the future. Considered purely from a sporting point of view an inflatable man-powered aircraft could be filled with a light gas, helium, in order to provide some buoyant lift. However, in the case of the 'Reluctant Phoenix' this would only have provided additional lift of the order of 10 lb. and so was probably not worth the expense. It is estimated that the power requirements for the 'Reluctant Phoenix' without resorting to the use of helium would only be ½ h.p. and so within the ability of many potential pilots. In terms of power saved by using a buoyant gas this could amount to 10% saving for this aircraft.

*Linnets I to V*

Returning to more conventional man-powered aircraft, 1965 saw the first man-powered flight in Japan with Linnet I. This was designed and built at Nihon University under the supervision of Professor Kimura who amongst other things is famous for designing the 'Zero' Second World War fighter. The design and construction of a man-powered aircraft was introduced as a postgraduate student project with Professor Kimura's class of ten students participating each year. To date this has resulted in Linnets I, II, III, IV, and V. The configuration of each is very similar, except for a major change from a reclining drive position of Linnet I to a cycling position for the later Linnets.

The Linnet series of man-powered aircraft consists of five distinctly separate aircraft although the design of each has been similar. This has been dictated by the lack of suitable hangars or runway at Nihon University until recently, such facilities now being available. This has meant that each Linnet had to be built, flown and then dismantled within a limited time scale at a separate airfield. It is surprising that under such conditions the Linnet aircraft were not designed to be trans-

*Linnets I* and *II*, showing the change from a reclining pilot position to a cycling position. *Prof. H. Kimura*

portable, as the practical limitations of this system prevented real development of the basic design.

Construction of all the Linnets consisted of a primary structure of spruce for the wing and tailplane, a welded metal truss for the fuselage and a lightweight but relatively fragile secondary structure of strip balsa covered with styrene paper, which appears to have been a stronger form of Japanese tissue paper. The incorporation of the spruce in the wing and tailplane construction was in the form of box beams with spruce in the top and bottom flanges separated by vertical balsa webs. The metal truss for the fuselage was constructed of thin gauge aluminium or steel tubing, both having been employed for different marks of Linnet, welded together with the attendant problem of warping of the structure. The propeller was made of glass-reinforced plastic on a framework of wooden stringers and ribs, the propeller having two blades utilising an R.A.F. 6 aerofoil section and being of 8.9 ft. diameter.

All the Linnets took-off under propeller thrust alone and take-off distances were of the order of 100 yards. Linnet I made several flights, the longest of which was 48 yards achieved in March, 1966. Later that year Linnet II was completed having the same wing design as the earlier aircraft but with the pilot in a cycling position instead of the reclining position. Also there were small detail differences arising from the experience gained with Linnet I, such as the propeller spinner that was used on I being eliminated for II and the later Linnets. Linnet II made 31 flights, the longest of 100 yards at a height of 5 ft. The two earlier Linnets, I and II, were sent to an exhibition in Italy and it is believed are on display in the Fiat Museum at Turin.

Linnet II was the most successful version to fly, probably because it was the only one on which it had been possible to do fairly extensive flight trials. Linnets III, IV and V all had wing spans increased to 83 ft. in order to improve the performance. In practice Linnet III made some eight flights, the longest being of 55 yards, before being dismantled. Linnet IV made only three or four flights over short distances before being destroyed when a gust caught it whilst on the ground. Linnet V was damaged during preliminary taxi-ing trials on the 18th March, 1972. Although the later Linnets were disappointing from a performance point of view, it must be stressed that they fulfilled their primary objective of being a useful and valid University student project. In addition Linnet IV is of interest as its controls were simplified to rudder and elevator alone. Ailerons were provided but only in the form of trim tabs, yet even with these modified controls the aircraft made successful take-offs and flights.

## Malliga Aircraft

Turning once more to Europe the next man-powered aircraft of note was that designed and built by Herr Josef Malliga of Austria. It is particularly interesting because it was designed and built by one man alone, which in itself is quite an achievement. However in this case Malliga went a stage further and designed the aircraft for simplicity of construction

Josef Malliga's first man-powered aircraft in flight at Zeltweg in Austria. *Josef Malliga*

and completely built the machine within 6 months.

Malliga, who is a jet-fighter flying instructor with the Austrian air force, first became interested in man-powered flight when he saw a programme on television describing the Kremer competition and the earlier British man-powered aircraft in flight. From that introduction, and spurred on by the £10,000 prize for the Kremer competition, Malliga decided to build his own machine. Although he had some knowledge of aerodynamics and the pilot position was determined by information contained in a pre-war German book, most of the design was carried out on the basis of 'what looks right is right'. This ad hoc basis is only valid if one has the necessary experience on which to base one's judgement and it is fortunate that in this case Malliga with his involvement in aviation did have the necessary experience.

A reclining position was chosen for the pilot from earlier information on the Haessler-Villinger aircraft and on the basis that it was a more natural piloting position. With the pilot's position chosen, the fuselage shape evolved in order to minimise the distance along the length of the drive mechanism to the propeller. The pilot's head emerged from the top of the fuselage to permit him to breathe effectively and the drag was reduced by the streamlined fairing behind the head. Drive to the propeller was by a horizontal shaft from bevel gears at the pedals directly to the propeller. The undercarriage was not driven because it was argued that a direct drive to the propeller with a high mechanical efficiency would be better in practice than a less efficient and heavier drive mechanism going via the undercarriage. In order to accommodate the propeller in the necessary position relative to the pilot the fuselage had to be mounted well above the ground. As the original propeller was of 6½ ft. diameter this meant that the fuselage had to be a minimum of 3 ft. off the ground.

The primary structure of the wing was an aluminium tube starting at 4 inch diameter at the centre and tapering to 1½ inch diameter at the outer section. The wing span came out to 64 ft. initially on the basis of the aluminium tubing that was available. Secondary structure was of expanded polystyrene as this was a lightweight material and could be easily worked. This was used in the form of 1 inch thick ribs, strengthened with a strip of thin plywood on one side of each rib. The leading edge was covered with sheet expanded polystyrene whilst the rest of the wing was covered with tissue paper, water-shrunk for tightness.

The aerodynamic design of the wing was also carried out on a rather ad hoc basis as Malliga created his own aerofoil section. He argued that previous aircraft had not complied with the requirements of the Kremer prize so that using their aerofoil sections would be inadequate. Therefore he designed his own by drawing it out freehand with about 20% thickness and correcting the shape until it 'looked right'. The fact that his machine has flown proved that Malliga's judgment was sound and may prove that man-powered aircraft aerodynamics are not as critical as had earlier been considered by aerodynamicists. Nevertheless it is interesting to speculate how well the aircraft would have performed if it had utilised the later more efficient aerofoil section used on Puffin II.

Controls consisted initially of elevator and transverse ailerons across the wing tips. Flight experience caused these to be modified and at an early stage the fin area was increased and rudders were added. It was also found that turns were difficult to achieve with the rudders provided, even with the comparatively small wing span involved, so paddle shaped spoilers were connected to the ailerons so that during a turn the inner one rotated at right angles to the airflow and thereby increased the drag of that wing tip.

The first flight was made in the autumn of 1967 and up till 1971 some forty flights had been made, most of them from towed launches behind a car. In fact the initial flight experience was gained with the pilot just handling the controls whilst being towed. The pilot for all the flights was Siegfried Puch who is an expert glider pilot and has the added advantage of weighing only 126 lb. in flying trim. Maximum flights achieved with the aircraft in its original form were about 400 yards from a towed launch and about 150 yards from a man-powered take-off. Take-off distances under man-power varied between 200 yards in still air conditions to as little as 130 yards in a light wind.

By the summer of 1971 Malliga had decided that the performance of his machine was inadequate and that improvements had to be made. His first approach was to make a new propeller of larger diameter since it was argued that increased diameter increased the swept area of the propeller and must therefore enhance thrust. This is valid but if the diameter is increased too much the drag of the propeller blades becomes too great for the man-power available. Diameter was increased from the original 6.5 ft. up to 9 ft. which is the usual maximum size for man-powered aircraft propellers. However, in this particular case this diameter was set as being the maximum that could be incorporated between the twin booms.

The new propeller design was again carried out in a fairly arbitrary manner because, not having any suitable criteria at the time on which to base it, Malliga made the blade shape the same as that employed for an old war time Russian Yak fighter aircraft to which he had access. The angle of attack was adjusted to give maximum static thrust with the pilot pedalling at his normal rate. On this basis the new propeller gave a static thrust, that is with the aircraft stationary, of over 30 lb. compared with 20 lb. for the original propeller.

Before trying the aircraft out with the new propeller, Malliga took the opportunity of increasing the wing span by adding two new 18 ft. wing panels, thereby increasing the effective wing span to 85 ft. The most interesting aspect of the new design is that the transverse ailerons have been superseded by more conventional ailerons which operate in a differential manner, being linked to both the aileron control and rudder control. With aileron control being exercised to

Malliga's aircraft with a modified wing during its disastrous first taxi trial. *Josef Malliga*

keep the aircraft level the ailerons operate in a conventional manner. However, when making turns with the rudder, the aileron at the inner wing tip moves to a vertical position and acts as a drag brake to aid the turn.

The modifications were completed by mid 1972 but one wing broke during taxi-ing trials due to a sudden side gust of wind. Repairs were completed and tension wires added to strengthen the outer wing panels. Flight trials recommenced during the Spring of 1973 and a flight of 328 yards was recorded during the summer of that year from a man-powered take-off.

### Dumbo

The next new design of man-powered aircraft to fly was the Weybridge group's 'Dumbo', so named because it had a wingspan of 120 ft., that is some 36 ft. greater than the span of Concorde. Design work started in 1967 under the leadership of Phil Green, a stress-man working at B.A.C. Weybridge, and nearly 10,000 man hours of construction time went into the aircraft before it flew in 1971. This very ambitious design

77

was based on such a large wingspan in order to improve the performance beyond that achieved by the earlier Southampton and Puffin British machines. Puffin II proved that a wingspan of 93 ft. was feasible and it was argued that from an aerodynamic point of view a wing span of 120 ft. was nearer the optimum. The theoretical power requirements were estimated at 0.3 h.p. for cruising flight which is a value that a fit man should be able to produce continuously for over an hour.

Construction of such a large wing required the solution of many difficult design problems. The weight had to be kept to a minimum but with a sufficiently stiff primary structure so as not to allow the wings to twist in flight and thereby lose the aerodynamic advantages of the long wings. Lateral controls were obviously essential with such large wings operating near the ground, but it was considered that the incorporation of ailerons would necessitate a much stronger and heavier structure to prevent aerodynamic twisting during their operation. The solution finally chosen was to allow the two wing halves to rotate relative to each other so that the angle of incidence of each could be varied in a manner similar to the method employed for the Haessler-Villinger machine. The primary structure of the wing was of thin gauge aluminium tubing joined by a fibre glass bonding technique originally suggested by Professor Czerwinski of the Canadian Aeronautics and Space Institute. The aluminium tubes were 0.010 inch thick, incorporated in the form of a box construction with four tubes at the corners held in position rigidly by tubular cross bracing. It was not possible to buy such thin gauge tubing off the shelf so all the tubing was originally bought at a thicker gauge and then had the excess material etched away, another advantage of being associated with the aircraft industry where such facilities are available. The wing primary structure was built on a jig and had a curvature put in to offset the droop of the wings under their own weight. It was designed so that when stationary there would still be adequate ground clearance under the bent wing and in flight

78

Close-up view of the *Dumbo*, showing the pilot position. The aircraft now renamed *Mercury*, is continuing flight trials at RAF Cranwell.
*Ron Moulton*

the wings would straighten out under the influence of the lift. It speaks well of the design that the wing structure behaved in practice more or less as it was supposed to do.

The secondary structure of the wing consisted of ribs spaced at one foot intervals and built of light balsa strip. These were built by individual members of the group in their homes and then assembled on to the primary structure in the hangar at Wisley Airfield. The ribs were made as light as possible in order to keep the wing weight down to a minimum. Although strong enough for the aerodynamic loading placed upon them, the ribs were made of such thin gauge balsa that they tended to deform under the tension of the 'Melinex' covering material, which meant that the final wing aerofoil section shape did not quite match up with that originally aimed at. Whilst it is debatable how critical aerofoil shapes are at the low speeds involved, nevertheless there must be some loss of performance due to the rib deformation. The

Weybridge group argued that this loss was probably small and therefore acceptable in view of the weight of the final wing. In view of the Malliga experience with his 'home grown' aerofoil section this is probably a valid argument.

The fuselage was also built up on an aluminium tubing structure joined by the same fibre glass bonding method as employed for the wing. This supported the all-moving tail surfaces which again had primary structures of aluminium tubing. Drive from the pilot, who operated in a reclining position with the control stick between his knees, was by chain to the drive wheel and by gearing and shaft to the propeller at the tail of the machine. The propeller was carved from balsa wood and has a fixed pitch, since it was argued that this would eliminate one possible source of trouble.

Construction of 'Dumbo' was started in 1968, the materials being bought by means of an £800 grant from the Royal Aeronautical Society. Major items were constructed at Wisley Airfield inside the hangar while smaller parts were made at group members' homes. Some of the more specialised parts were turned out at the Rolls-Royce Technical College, Filton, and the Derby College of Further Education. It will be apparent that a great deal of effort went into the construction of this machine, and, as stated earlier, some 10,000 man hours were put in before the aircraft was ready for flight trials late in 1970. The initial taxi-ing trials showed that the angle of

*Dumbo* during its maiden flight at Brooklands, Weybridge, piloted by Chris Lovell, September 18th 1971. *Bristol Aircraft Corporation*

incidence was too small and this was modified early in 1971. A further set-back occurred in March 1971 when, having wheeled the aircraft out on to the runway for further taxi-ing trials, a 12 knot gust of wind suddenly came along and turned it over. This damaged several of the ribs and the fin, but fortunately did not damage the primary structure of the machine. After repairs the aircraft then had to be moved from Wisley to the main B.A.C. airfield at Weybridge, where the Company made a hangar available.

The first flight was made on the 18th September, 1971, when the pilot extended taxi-ing trials up to take-off speed and the machine lifted off about a foot above the runway for about 30 yards. The next flight was of 50 yards at 3ft. above the runway. Following the directional control problems experienced during those two flights by the pilot Chris Lovell, an experienced glider pilot as well as a cyclist, the opportunity was taken to modify the rudder and also to increase the size of the propeller from its original 7 ft. diameter. The Weybridge group had no further opportunity to fly and a group at Cranwell under the leadership of Flight Lieutenant John Potter, who earlier flew the Jupiter man-powered aircraft, has taken over its development. Flight Lieutenant Potter was confident that the control problems could be solved both on the basis of his experience with Jupiter and through a computer simulation of the Dumbo control characteristics. This confidence was further strengthened when he got it a few inches into the air during taxi-ing trials on the 10th July, 1974.

The Cranwell group has renamed the aircraft 'Mercury', so following the tradition of using the names of planets started with the Jupiter man-powered aircraft.

*Jupiter*

'Jupiter', the next British man-powered aircraft to fly, was originally started by the Woodford group under the leadership of the designer Chris Roper in 1964. The only man-powered aircraft to have flown then were the Southampton and Puffin I machines and it is easy to see how 'Jupiter' incorporates some of the lessons learnt from those aircraft. 'Jupiter' had a similar conventional layout to SUMPAC but with the improved cycling pilot position of Puffin I. Chris Roper continued with the construction of the aircraft on an individual basis until it was partially destroyed in a fire in his workshop during 1969. The machine was then taken over by a group at the R.A.F. Apprentice Training School at Halton under the leadership of Flt. Lt. John Potter. They repaired all the damaged parts and completed construction by late 1971, the first flight being made on 13th February, 1972.

The design of 'Jupiter' is interesting since much of it is conventional in terms of the materials employed, namely spruce and balsa wood for the structure, and configuration. The wing span is only 79ft. yet it holds the present record for man-powered flight. This can be attributed partly to the wing construction which is the cleanest, the term being employed in the aerodynamic sense, ever to have been built into a man-powered aircraft. Ribs are spaced at only 3 inches apart along the length in order to preserve a consistent aerodynamic profile. External strips of balsa wood are employed with each rib to ensure that the covering material adheres correctly to the under camber of the section. The primary structure has been stiffened to ensure that the wing does not twist under aerodynamic loading and the wing constitutes much of the 145 lb. weight of this comparatively heavy machine. Surprisingly the aerofoil section used is a fairly early low drag profile having a 'paper' performance below that employed for even the early machines such as SUMPAC or Puffin I. It would have been interesting to see how 'Jupiter' would have performed with the later more advanced aerofoil sections.

Drive and propulsion of 'Jupiter' represent a break with tradition as the drive is by chain only, whilst the propeller is a low speed, wide chord type similar to that used for rubber powered aeromodels. The pilot operates the pedals from a cycling position, drive being taken back to a layshaft just behind the undercarriage wheel from where a chain drive is taken directly up to the propeller and another chain drive goes forward to the drive wheel. Renold chain of 3/32 inch width is used throughout and the system appears to be both reliable and efficient, and is of interest to the home constructor of man-powered aircraft as the parts are readily available and comparatively inexpensive. The propeller is built up on an aluminium tube with balsa ribs and has a diameter of about 8 ft. with a chord of nearly 12 inches.

Controls are conventional: ailerons, rudder and an all-flying tailplane. The tailplane was controlled by a twistgrip on the handlebars and was all-flying which made if fairly difficult to control in practice. Anyway the pilot, John Potter, found that he tended to over-control in the longitudinal direction during the early flights with a subsequent loss of performance. However flying experience and the incorporation of a device for showing the angle of incidence of the aircraft have enabled these problems to be overcome.

Much of the performance of 'Jupiter' can be attributed directly to the fact that the pilot had more flying experience with it within a relatively short period than had been the case with any other man-powered aircraft. Furthermore he was an experienced pilot of more conventionally powered aircraft before starting flight trials with 'Jupiter' and this, he feels, is invaluable for any such endeavour. His thesis is that the pilot of a man-powered aircraft must function with his body operating in two different modes, the upper half geared to control whilst the lower half must be geared to the motive power. Certainly the fact that on the 60th flight with 'Jupiter' on the 29th May, 1972, he recorded a flight of 1711 yards in length and thereby set a new record for man-powered aircraft adds much evidence to his views. Within those 60 flights John Potter had amassed approximately one hour of flying time, which on the face of it seems a small amount yet,

*Jupiter* in flight at RAF Benson, 1972, in which John Potter made his record ¾ mile flight. *Crown*

in terms of the four-month period over which it was gained, makes it by far the most concentrated man-powered flying ever achieved to date. This enabled him to learn from each flight thereby building up experience consistently, unlike the pilots of previous aircrafts who had sufficient time between flights to forget the lessons learnt on the earlier attempts.

Flt. Lt. Potter has developed a technique of controlling 'Jupiter' by using the rudder and ailerons as separate controls rather than interlinking them for turns as with more conventional aircraft. Although only straight flights have at present been tried with 'Jupiter' the necessary turns required to keep it on course are made with the rudder whilst the ailerons are simply used to maintain the aircraft on a level keel. During earlier flights the rudder and ailerons were used together and resulted in 'dutch-rolling', a term derived from the ice skating on the canals of Holland and implying a combined roll and yawing motion of the aircraft. Admittedly the moment arm of the fuselage on 'Jupiter' is greater than on previous man-powered aircraft and this must result in more effective operation of the rudder.

The earlier flights of 'Jupiter' were of short duration but as John Potter gained more experience with the machine the flight durations have increased. Recorded best flight is that mentioned above of 1171 yards in length although an unofficial flight of about 1350 yards has been achieved, the latter flight being terminated only by runway restrictions at R.A.F. Benson where the aircraft is flown. It was found that earlier the aircraft had been flown at too great an angle of incidence, i.e. at too low a flying speed, but the later, more successful flights were at the correct angle for the optimum lift/drag ratio. The initial flight trials of 'Jupiter' were terminated as John Potter attended a post graduate course at the University of London in 1972/73 and the aircraft was stored during his absence. Since then he has taken a post at Cranwell and continued man-powered flight development with both 'Jupiter' and 'Mercury'.

Original three-bladed
propeller on the Peter
Wright aircraft.
*Author's collection*

### Wright aircraft

At about the same time that 'Jupiter' was being flown
another British man-powered aircraft was making its first
flight — an individual project by Peter Wright that he had
built and financed entirely on his own with the Kremer
Prize as the ultimate objective. Started in mid-1971 the
aircraft involved 500 hours of construction time and made
its first flight in February, 1972. Peter Wright, who is a design
engineer with a production engineering research establishment, designed the aircraft for ease of production and was
obviously very successful in view of the short time required
between the start and finish of the project. His approach was
to reduce both the weight and the construction time by
minimising the structure of the aircraft. This he did by
utilising carbon fibres to reinforce the basic wooden structure.

The *Wright* man-powered aircraft showing later modifications to the rear fuselage and propeller. *Ron Moulton*

Carbon fibres, which is really a composite material of a plastic matrix reinforced with carbon fibres, has exceptionally good strength and stiffness properties for a low density. This was the reason for its use, or at least its tentative use, for the fan blades on jet engines. However it is slowly coming into more widespread use for general industrial purposes, and although the price is still fairly high it is no longer prohibitive for man-powered aircraft applications. It is possible to buy low grade carbon fibres that are perfectly adequate for such applications for as little as £15 per lb. When it is remembered that with the high strength of carbon fibres only a few lb. would be needed for any particular aircraft, the cost is justifiable. The Wright aircraft, for example, incorporates only 7 lb. of carbon fibres.

The Wright aircraft has a total weight of 90 lb. and the lowest wing loading of any man-powered aircraft to date (see Table 1). Wright considers that with more care during the construction the empty weight could have been reduced to 60 lb., the extra 30 lb. being largely taken up by the pilot support frame which is constructed of steel tubing. The most amazing part of the aircraft weight was the wing weight, which for most man-powered aircraft is the heaviest unit of the machine, but with this aircraft only weighed 20 lb. altogether. This involved an expanded polystyrene (EPS) and balsa primary structure reinforced by carbon fibres with lightweight strip balsa ribs spaced at every 2 ft. The wing started life with a 60 ft. span, but having heard about all the very large wing spans being used for other man-powered aircraft, Peter Wright decided to increase the wing span to 71 ft. before the initial flight trials by the addition of small wing units at the original wing tips. As the aircraft did not have ailerons it was also considered that the wing tip units could be used for trimming if necessary. The wing tip units did not have the same constructional form as the original wing, being made entirely of E.P.S. reinforced with carbon fibres.

The fuselage consisted of a 'pod and boom' lay-out constructed of a minimal wooden structure reinforced with carbon fibres. The pilot operated from a semi-reclining position, sitting and pedalling, the drive being taken via a chain and shaft system to a 6 ft. diameter three-bladed propeller at the tail. Controls were to have been rudder and elevator but the aircraft made its first few flights using rudder alone, as Peter Wright wished to fly before installing the elevator controls. As he had not previously flown, he considered that the rudder would be enough to handle. Stemming from aeromodelling practice the aircraft was not designed with ailerons, another reason that the wing weight was so low, and to provide stability during the take-off run the aircraft was equipped with a tricycle undercarriage. This consisted of the drive wheel at the front and two small trailing wheels aft of the pod part of the fuselage.

The first flight was made in February, 1972, at Langer airfield near Nottingham, where the aircraft was assembled, having been constructed at Peter Wright's home and then transported in a furniture van. It is interesting to note that the aircraft was designed in sections with such transportation in mind and this obviously placed further restrictions on the aircraft configuration that other man-powered aircraft have not been subjected to. The aircraft flew for 200 yards at about a foot above the runway during the first flight with Peter Wright at the controls. Unfortunately the elevator was not set quite correctly and the drive wheel came off the runway before the aircraft had attained flying speed and the take-off run was completed on propeller thrust alone. Since then several flights have been made, the longest being about 300 yards in length with altitudes of up to 4 ft. above the runway. All flights were made without elevator so that the climb could only be accomplished by an increase in power.

With the very low wing loading of the Wright aircraft it could be flown only in very calm conditions and all the flights were made near dusk on calm evenings. Since the limitations in flying conditions must obviously have a major effect on any attempt at the Kremer prize it is interesting to note Peter Wright's practical solution to the problem. The weather is normally much calmer during the night and if the wind was too strong during the hours of daylight, then he was prepared to fly at night by artificial light from car headlights. There is nothing in the Kremer competition regulations to prohibit this. However, development of the aircraft was terminated in the summer of 1973 when Peter Wright had to vacate the airfield at Langer.

## Liverpuffin

The third British man-powered aircraft to fly in 1972 was the Liverpuffin, designed and built by students of the department of Mechanical Engineering at Liverpool University. This project was started in the autumn of 1969 as part of the students' course in engineering design. This use of man-powered aircraft as a student exercise will be discussed in more detail in Chapter 6. Design is aimed at the production of an end product that MUST work, and the basic idea of this particular project was to provide a challenge whereby the complete design process had to be adhered to. The Hatfield group heard about this project and offered the remains of the crashed Puffin II which otherwise would have lain idle. These were gratefully accepted and the name of Puffin was retained for the new aircraft although it was changed to Liverpuffin in view of the new configuration, aims and venue.

At an early stage of the design process it was decided, with some regret on the part of the students, that the Kremer prize was beyond the scope of such a machine. Other criteria were therefore chosen and these were that the aircraft should be robust, otherwise considerable time would be spent on repairs, transportable and stable in flight. Transportability was necessary because the aircraft had to be built in the University and flown at an airfield at least 20 miles away. The aircraft had to be manageable to be suitable for a wide range of potential pilots and to be capable of being flown in reasonable wind conditions, otherwise flying would be very restricted especially near the north west coast of England.

These criteria required that the wing span should be fairly small and the wing loading high. At the start of the project information was available regarding only the Southampton and Puffin machines and it was originally decided to make the wing span 68 ft. but subsequently, in view of the success of the Malliga aircraft, it was reduced to 64 ft. During construction the weight went up from an estimated 125 lb. to 140 lb., a typical increase for such a project, which with the author as pilot resulted in the very high wing loading of nearly 1 lb./sq. ft. In view of the equally high wing loading of Jupiter this should not be as detrimental to performance as it was originally thought to be in the early '60s.

Parts from Puffin II incorporated in this machine included the pilot support frame, propeller, primary wing structure after being suitably repaired, and the tail surfaces, again after being repaired. This meant the construction of a new fuselage and wing secondary structure together with the provision of new controls. It was decided to eliminate the ailerons as it was considered that the incorporation of a large dihedral angle for the wings would make the aircraft laterally stable. This decision aroused some criticism from the pundits. They agreed that in free air conditions the aircraft would be stable, but not during the take-off run. However the decision was adhered to and in view of experience of Linnet IV and the Wright machine it was justified, although knowledge regarding these aircraft did not come to hand until just before Liverpuffin made its first flight. Elimination of ailerons had several advantages, simplification of the wing structure and easing of the pilot's control problem being the major ones. It was argued that the pilot would have sufficient to do in propelling the aircraft without needing to manage a lot of complex controls. Controls were to have been rudder and elevator but the aircraft eventually made its first flight using rudder alone.

The fuselage was of a functional design incorporating a 'pod and boom' layout, the pilot being housed in the pod and the tubular aluminium boom carrying the tail surfaces. This type of layout was decided upon because of the simpler construction and because the moment arm could be increased above that of Puffin to make the rudder operation more effective without incurring either major weight penalties or additional construction time. The propeller was mounted just behind the pod, making the distance that the drive had to be taken shorter than with the Puffins. Control wires for the rudder were carried from a handle bar at the front of the pod back to the rudder through the boom.

The most interesting innovation in Liverpuffin was the secondary structure of the wing. When searching for a form that would reduce constructional time and also make a robust structure it was decided that expanded polystyrene would be the ideal material not only because of its low density but also because of its ability to withstand shock loading. A form of construction utilising an expanded polystyrene shell with lightening holes and stiffening ribs at every 18 inches was chosen. This was used for the centre part of the wing because it had a constant chord and therefore only one set of templates for wire cutting the expanded polystyrene would be required. It was originally intended to continue this form of construction for the two outer wings, but as they tapered and templates would be required for each expanded polystyrene unit it was decided that construction time for both the templates and polystyrene units would be prohibitive. Sheet balsa ribs made in low density balsa wood, 3/16 inch thick, spaced at 1 foot intervals were eventually used for the outer wings. The weight penalty associated with these sheet ribs compared with built up balsa strip ribs was small, as the total weight of the outer wing sections, each being of 17 ft. span, was only 30 lb., yet they were very much easier to construct.

The aircraft was completed in December 1971, and made its first taxi-ing trials on the 16th December, in a 5 knot wind along a short stretch of taxi-way, the main runway being occupied. Small initial problems were then ironed out with the aim of making a flight attempt on the 17th, this being a good day for first flights, going right back to the Wright brothers in 1903. However, when the aircraft was wheeled out on to the runway on the 17th in a 5 knot wind, a sudden gust of 15 knots came along that took the handlers by surprise and turned the aircraft completely over on to its back. The results were not as disastrous as they might have been, most of the damage being concentrated on the outer wing sections, one propeller blade and the tailplane, which was a complete write-off. It speaks well of the robust construction of the aircraft that repairs took only two months to complete.

The tailplane reconstruction utilised expanded polystyrene

The author surrounded by the crashed remains of *Liverpuffin*, December 1971. *Author's collection*

with a tube through each half of the tailplane to take the bending loads. This proved to be as light as the original Puffin tailplane which was made throughout of balsa wood, but involved a mere 15 hours of construction time. Fortunately it was possible to reassemble the bits of the propeller blade and stick them together, both blades then being given a thin coat of fibre glass to improve the strength.

The aircraft was ready for flying again by March, 1972, but by then an invitation had been received to take it to the United States for exhibition, and to avoid any possibility of damage it was decided to limit flight trials to conditions when the wind strength was no greater than 5 knots. Several days were spent waiting for suitable conditions and eventually these were obtained on the 18th March, 1972. With the author as pilot the aircraft managed to get to the stage of just hopping off the runway on the first tow runs, indicating that the aircraft was up to take-off speed but that there was insufficient thrust from the propeller to maintain flight. After some adjustments to the tailplane and propeller settings a short flight of about 20 yards at a height of about 9 inches was achieved, proving conclusively that the aircraft would fly. The propeller was still not adjusted correctly but by the time that had been done the wind had increased to 8 knots and a further

The rebuilt *Liverpuffin* on display above the statue of Benjamin Franklin at the Franklin Institute, Philadelphia. *Author's collection*

attempt was not risked.

No other opportunity to fly was available before the aircraft had to be packed up for shipment to the States in April. The aircraft was subsequently exhibited in the States at Transpo '72 where it created so much interest and enthusiasm that it was retained for further display at the Franklin and Smithsonian Institutions.

*Toucan*

The last man-powered aircraft to fly in 1972 was Toucan, a two man machine constructed by the Hertfordshire Pedal Aeronauts, who were originally associated with the Handley-Page Aircraft Company before the company was disbanded.

This aircraft represents a major achievement on the part of the group because the association with the Handley-Page Company caused set-backs in the construction programme whilst the aircraft itself was the largest and most complex

94

man-powered aircraft to fly up till that time. Furthermore, Toucan is the first two man machine to fly.

Two man machines had been discussed before the first SUMPAC flight on the basis that one man can concentrate on the piloting whilst the other produces most of the power. One previous two man machine was built but never flown, the Southend 'Mayfly', with which Martin Pressnell, leader of the Hertfordshire group, was associated.

Pressnell had stated that the two man arrangement was chosen since it seemed to offer a better power-weight ratio and the prospect of improved power continuity compared with a single seater. Certainly with original target weight of 145 lb. empty these points were valid but in practice the weight increased for the 123 ft. wing span aircraft.

Structural design was based on a simple space frame constructed of spruce and balsa wood, spruce being used for the wing span booms and fuselage longerons for instance, so that the aircraft could be split in several sub-assemblies. This simplified the construction and allowed it to take place within a workshop 66 ft. x 21 ft., erected by the group on ground provided by Handley-Page at Radlett.

This demonstrates the size of the *Toucan*, a two-man machine, here shown with its original span of 123ft. which was later increased to 139ft. *Ron Moulton*

It was anticipated that novel solutions would be required to overcome the control problems of such a large aircraft. A wing tip deflection of 7½ ft. was calculated at the design stage which with a small built-in dihedral would help lateral stability. In practice an actual deflection of 12 ft. was measured so that the aircraft was modified to reduce the original dihedral angle. A rudder was not incorporated but following the Puffin II experience wing tip slot-lip ailerons were provided to aid turns. It was reasoned that the elimination of a rudder would reduce the rear fuselage weight and also avoid flow disturbances in the region of the propeller.

The aircraft was completed in the summer of 1972, and taxi-ing trials were carried out at the old Handley-Page airfield at Radlett. Speed was increased until the aircraft hopped off the ground but would not fly. It was thought that the propeller was not correctly adjusted to the airspeed and that

The *Toucan* during its successful 700yd. flight, July 1973, at the old Handley Page airfield, Radlett. *Ron Moulton*

it was preventing flight. The next trial was performed without the propeller and the aircraft accelerated up to take-off speed, rose into the air for about a foot then glided back to ground, proving conclusively that the propeller pitch had previously been at fault.

Following adjustments to the propeller, Toucan made its first flight on the 23rd December, 1972, with Bryan Bowan as pilot and Derek May as the other crew member. Out of three flights made on that day the longest was measured at 68 yards at a height of 2 ft. Since then a flight of 700 yards lasting for 1 minute 18 seconds and during which a height of 15 feet was observed, was recorded on the 3rd July, 1973. Unfortunately it ended in disaster as a failure of one wing occurred and the aircraft was badly damaged. At least 12 months' repair work was anticipated but the group was determined to complete the reconstruction and utilise the time spent on the work more effectively by increasing the wingspan to 139 feet.

*Hurel Aviette*

Maurice Hurel has long been an advocate of high lift, high aspect ratio wings for use in aircraft design. Man-powered flight provides an ideal application for this form of construction and the result is the Hurel Aviette.

With a wing span of 132 ft. it is the largest single seat man-powered aircraft to have flown, being 12 ft. longer than Dumbo. The construction is of spruce and balsa wood and represents 3 years' work. In order to keep the weight down to a minimum, a parasol wing with external bracing has been used. Controls are conventional with lateral control provided by ailerons. To prevent the long high aspect wing twisting due to the aerodynamic loading during ailerons operation, out-rigger auxiliary aerofoils are attached to the wing and are fitted behind the trailing edge.

The whole aircraft embodies unusual design features, one

The *Hurel Aviette* during initial gliding trials at le Bourget. *Maurice Hurel*

The 132ft. span *Hurel Aviette* with Maurice Hurel and the pilot, J. Pierre Thierrard. *Ron Moulton*

of the most noticeable being a tractor propeller of 10 ft. diameter at the nose of the aircraft. All other man-powered aircraft have employed pusher propellers in order to minimise drag by not having any part of the aircraft in the high speed slipstream leaving the propeller. There are several advantages in using a tractor propeller in that it simplifies the drive mechanism from the pilot. Also the airstream entering the propeller is uninterrupted at the nose of the aircraft and so could improve efficiency. Unfortunately one practical disadvantage of a tractor propeller is that it is more susceptible to damage at the front of the aircraft. This was shown on the fourth flight, when the propeller was broken.

As Maurice Hurel was in his mid 70's at the time of the initial flight trials he has not been able to pilot the aircraft himself. However, he was able to check on the control characteristics personally during initial towed trials behind a car. Unfortunately the flying must be restricted to very light wind conditions due to the low wing loading and this has restricted the flight experience with the aircraft.

# 4

# Design
# considerations

It is proposed to discuss briefly the design considerations involved with man-powered aircraft. In no way does this chapter set out to provide detailed design data as this has been provided in the previous book by the author, "Man Powered Flight".

The aspect of man-powered flight that makes it so challenging is that it relies on man power alone. Whereas a glider, which is the nearest equivalent to a man-powered aircraft, requires the equivalent of probably 4 h.p., a man-powered aircraft has to rely on a maximum of about ½ h.p. Man's power output comes from two sources, from chemical energy released during the oxidation of food and from reactions within the muscles. The oxidation energy output is steady and simply depends on the amount of oxygen that can be absorbed. Output from oxidation has been quoted as being about 0.4 h.p. for a fit young man, and as high as 0.54 h.p. for Olympic athletes. The additional power derived from hydrolytic reactions within the muscles varies according to the duration of the exercise and values of as high as 2 h.p. have been quoted for durations of about 5 seconds.

In practice these values appear to be rather optimistic as tests performed by the author in connection with the Liverpuffin project on male students at Liverpool University indicated that most could achieve a power output of ½ h.p. if only for a few seconds, but that few could achieve powers of 0.6 h.p. These tests were performed on a cycling rig which was supposed to simulate the requirements of the aircraft. Also it was noted that power output varied considerably from day to day, or even during a given day. As a case in point the author, who has a weight of 160 lb. but is not a cyclist, has produced outputs ranging from 0.6 h.p. for up to 30 seconds, down as low as 0.5 h.p. for only 5 seconds. Furthermore it has been noticed that for a given person higher outputs were generally obtained during the morning than in the afternoon.

Obviously a static test rig within the laboratory cannot give completely valid performance data because in the actual aircraft there would be a psychological urge to get airborne or to extend one's flight. However it does appear that a realistic maximum power requirement for any man-powered aircraft would be ½ h.p., and it is worthy of note that this is the value upon which the design of SUMPAC was based.

For extending power outputs above this level it is possible to think in terms of trained athletes, although this would limit the general appeal of man-powered flight. Alternatively, additional power can be produced by combined pedalling and hand cranking. Ursinus performed some tests before the war in connection with the German interest in man-powered aircraft. He concluded that pedalling and hand cranking together yielded about 50% more power than just cycling alone, although for only short durations of under 5 minutes. In practice his other power predictions appear to be optimistic, so that if one were to use both the arms and legs for power production it would be safer to assume a lower improvement figure of say 25% – 30%.

Up to the present time nobody has tried combined pedalling and hand cranking in an actual man-powered aircraft since the pilot is required to have his arms free for control purposes. There is a two seater project where the second crew member would use his arms as well as his legs for power production. This is the 'Flycycle' being built by students at the Northrop Institute of Technology in America. Although this has yet to be completed and tried out in practice, power tests have been carried out on the crew that are very encouraging.

However, if one thinks in terms of the combined use of legs and arms, or of leg power alone, the major problem of man-powered flight is the lack of power. Even the Wright brothers had several horse power to play with whilst man's output is appreciably less than one horse power. This means that the designer of a man-powered aircraft has to ensure that the resistance to motion, in other words the 'drag', and the speed are as low as possible.

Let us take as an example a motor car. This is within everyone's experience and is a classic illustration of the effect of drag and speed on power. The motion of a car is resisted by the friction within the mechanical parts and also by friction between the wheels and the road. On top of these there is an additional resistance, commonly described as wind resistance, which is the drag. In order to make a particular car go faster it must be streamlined. This is why fast cars, especially sports cars, have a low rakish appearance. By making them low the frontal area is decreased and by streamlining them the airflow round them is improved and the drag thereby reduced.

We can take our analogy of the car a stage further because we know from direct experience that the faster one travels the more power is required. If there is limited power then the speed is also limited. Hence, it can be seen that with a man-powered aircraft the low power means that both speed and drag must be minimised. Unfortunately these two factors are interrelated, as a decrease in speed means that the wing size must be increased to maintain lift, but a larger wing has greater drag than a smaller one.

As with most design problems the final solution must be a compromise chosen on the basis of additional requirements. If maximum performance is required and this is judged to mean that the man's power level must be reduced in order that the power can be maintained for a longer duration, then the resulting design has maximum practical wing size. Such aircraft as 'Dumbo' and 'Toucan' were thought to represent the maximum practical size of wing, but now they have flown successfully the question of how far wing spans can be increased above 139 ft. has still to be answered.

On the other hand, if simplicity of control and construction are taken as the necessary criteria, the resulting design would correspond to the smaller type of man-powered aircraft, such as 'Liverpuffin'.

It is noticeable that all the practical man-powered aircraft that have so far flown are 'conventional' in that they are fixed wing monoplanes having possibly unusual but nevertheless recognisable conventional features such as a fuselage, tailplane and fin. However, there is a school of thought with a many adherents which suggests that if one has limited power it can be utilised more effectively by putting that power directly into the lifting mechanism of the aircraft, either in the form of flapping wings or as a helicopter.

Without necessarily disagreeing with this point of view there are valid reasons why such devices are not practical at the present state of the art. A helicopter, for example, has advantages over a fixed wing aircraft for man-powered flight only if the rotor and fuselage assembly can be made much smaller and more easily. Unfortunately the smaller the helicopter rotor the more power is required for a given amount of lift. For a helicopter simply to hover using only man-power the rotor would need to have a minimum diameter of 60 ft. situated at a height of 4 ft. above the ground. The consequence

103

Bob Wilson's autogyro, showing a very individual, but unfortunately unsuccessful, approach to man-powered flight. *Royal Aeronautical Society*

Assembling the parts of the *'Flycycle'* a man-powered autogyro, is the designer Mr. H.R. Barnard. Interesting features include a ducted propeller for improved propulsion. Although construction was started in the 1960's there has been no record of either completion or flight trials. *Author's collection*

of a large flexible rotor rotating at a small distance above the ground can well be imagined. Several smaller diameter rotor helicopters have been built for man-powered flight but none has left the ground.

On the question of flapping wings the problem is less clear cut. For example, the exponents maintain that one should look to nature for the optimum solution to any problem and that in this case flapping wings are the ideal choice. They combine two functions, those of lift and propulsion, whilst conventional aircraft require two separate mechanisms for these.

The opponents are more concerned with the arguments rather than the merits or otherwise of flapping wings. They state that if nature always comes up with the best solution then cars would be walking around on legs rather than running on wheels. Nature, they maintain, is limited by the reciprocating motions necessary to get power from muscles. Man on the other hand can utilise rotating equipment which in the case of man-powered aircraft means a propeller for propulsion.

The truth is that nobody knows. There is certainly some basis for thinking that flapping wings might be more efficient than fixed wings as the very flapping motion modifies the air flow round the wing and reduces drag. However, we do not understand the flapping motions sufficiently well to design even a small flapping wing let alone a 60 ft. span wing suitable for a small man-powered aircraft. Until the necessary research has been performed this question is one of speculation and therefore outside the scope of practical man-powered aircraft.

Hence we are left with the use of conventional fixed wing aircraft for man-powered flight within the foreseeable future. However, even within this restriction there is still plenty of scope for design ingenuity as there is for a choice of configuration. This is well illustrated in the previous chapter because, although the aircraft described there could be loosely termed conventional monoplanes they were of different

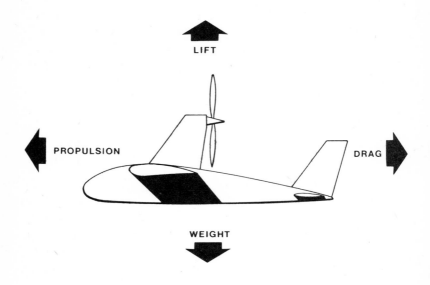

*Figure 8.* Forces on an aircraft.

shapes and sizes and accordingly had different aims. Further variations can be introduced, either monoplanes or biplanes for example. In order to discuss these choices in more detail one has to appreciate the basic aerodynamics of the problem.

A man-powered aircraft is subject to four basic forces which are illustrated in Figure 8. Weight is an inherent part of the aircraft and in order to fly must be overcome by the lift. However to produce lift from a wing it has to move through the air and by doing so there is a resistance to its motion which takes the form of drag. Finally there must be a propulsive force, which in the case of man-powered aircraft is provided by the propeller, in order to overcome the drag so that the aircraft can move forward at its necessary speed.

The lift from a wing is a function of its size — as defined by the wing span and chord — its speed through the air and its cross-sectional shape. In order to produce lift the wing section must be so shaped as to create a high pressure region of air below the wing and a low pressure region above. However, the shape of the wing section not only affects the lift but also the drag.

Drag of a wing section is dependant on two types of resistance to motion, the skin friction and the wake behind the section. Skin friction is determined by the behaviour of the air flow near the surface of the wing and by the roughness of the actual wing surface. This is why Melinex covering is ideal for man-powered aircraft as it is light yet provides a very smooth surface.

Any object flowing through air or water has a wake behind it. As the wing passes through the air, the air has to separate to go round it and then rejoin at the trailing edge of the wing. This rejoining is never perfect and there is always some mixing of two airstreams from either side of the wing, resulting in eddies being formed. Eddies require energy to be given by the wing to the airflow for their formation and this shows up in practice as a form of drag. The larger the wake formed, the greater the drag.

Care has to be taken with the design of wing sections for man-powered aircraft in order to ensure that high lift is produced for low drag. The creation of the wake behind the wing is most critical as it is affected by the behaviour of the airflow over the front of the wing. If the airflow over the front is modified by a change in wing section shape in an endeavour to produce more lift it will modify the drag. The necessary knowledge required to allow the development of wing sections suitable for man-powered aircraft stemmed from early experience with gliders. In a search for improved glider performance a considerable amount of research has been carried out on wing sections so that there has been a general improvement in the wing sections available to man-powered

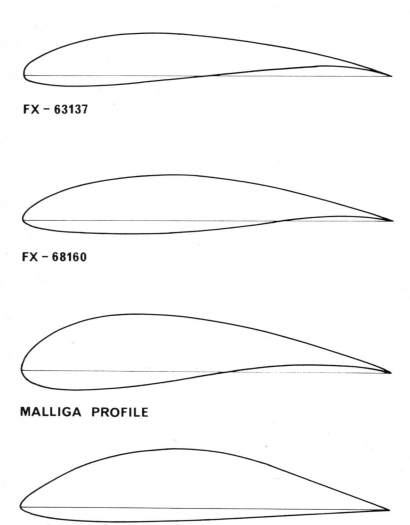

**FX – 63137**

**FX – 68160**

**MALLIGA PROFILE**

**GU 25 – 5 (11) 8**

*Figure 9.* Four modern man-powered aircraft wing sections.

aircraft.

This can be appreciated by comparing the lift/drag ratio for the wing sections used on three man-powered aircraft:

| | First Flight | Lift Coefficient | Wing Section L/D |
|---|---|---|---|
| Haessler-Villinger | 1935 | 1.1 | 70 |
| Puffin I | 1961 | 0.8 | 90 |
| Puffin II | 1965 | 1.15 | 125 |

The lift coefficient is a value assigned to the lift-producing ability of a particular section shape. It will be appreciated that up to the early 60's there was a general improvement of the performance of wing sections but at the expense of a decrease in the lift. With the introduction of the wing section used for Puffin II the new generation of sections provides a real improvement in terms of both lift and L/D ratio.

Figure 9 shows four modern wing sections suitable for man-powered aircraft. The FX-63137 used for Puffin II and Liverpuffin, and the FX-68160 used for Dumbo were both developed by Dr. Wortmann of Stuttgart University, who has had considerable success with wing sections developed for modern high performance gliders. The significance of the numerals is that the first two represent the year, 1963 and 1968 respectively, whilst the last three represent the thickness of the section with relation to the chord. Malliga used the third section shown for his man-powered aircraft. Its development was on the ad-hoc basis and the profile shown in Figure 7 is only an approximate reproduction of the true wing section as no record was retained of the actual shape. The final wing section, the GU 25-5(11)8, was the result of a theoretical computer study made by Professor Nonweiler of Glasgow University for a very high lift section.

Fortunately there are sufficient performance data to allow

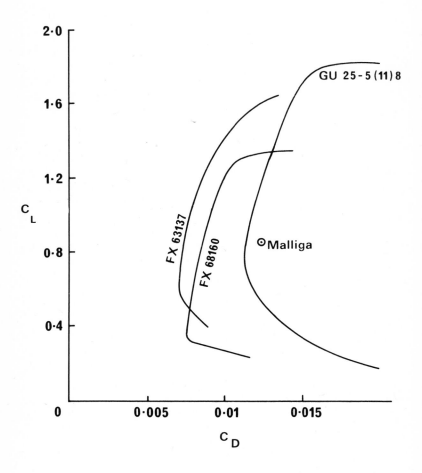

*Figure 10.* Lift/drag characteristics for four wing sections.

a comparison of these four sections. Figure 10 shows a plot of the lift/drag characteristics appropriate to man-powered aircraft.* The graphs for the FX-63137 and GU 25-5(11)8 are based upon wind tunnel tests and in the case of the FX-63137 the validity of these results has been confirmed by its use on Puffin II and Liverpuffin. The graph for the FX-68160 is one estimated by the Weybridge group for its use with Dumbo. Flight trials with this aircraft have provided some confirmation of the validity of their estimation. One point is shown for the Malliga profile, this being an estimation of its actual performance within the aircraft.

It would appear on the basis of Figure 10, that the Wortmann FX-63137 has still the best performance of any available wing section suitable for man-powered flight. Certainly the more recent GU 25-5(11)8 provides greater lift but at the expense of increased drag, this probably being a function of the thicker section. The Malliga profile has a fairly classic high lift shape which does not seem to have been fully utilised in practice, whilst the drag is very high. In fact the estimated lift/drag ratio for the Malliga wing section is 77 which is only 10% better than that for the pre-war Haessler-Villinger aircraft. From this one is left wondering how much better the aircraft might have performed with an improved wing section. On the other hand the section was simply drawn out by hand and yet still provided a good performance when compared to those wing sections available a mere decade ago.

Choice of a wing section does not rest entirely on its aerodynamic performance as the wing must also house a structure to provide the necessary strength. The deeper a structure the greater strength can be achieved for a given weight, so that from a strength point of view the wing section should be as deep as possible. The FX-63137 is not necessarily

* In technical terms the plots are at a Reynolds number of 700,000

the ideal section as it is only 13.7% thick with relation to the chord. A better compromise between the structural and aerodynamic requirement is probably the FX-68160 which is 16% thick, although some of the earlier man-powered aircraft have employed wing sections of 18% thickness. One final advantage of the FX-68160 over the FX-63137 is its simpler shape. The latter has a finely tapered trailing edge which is difficult to construct in practice.

Having chosen a wing section for a man-powered aircraft this is only one of the designer's problems solved, as he has to minimise the drag of the total aircraft. This means taking care over the streamlining over the fuselage and is the reason for the pilots of man-powered aircraft being encased in enclosed cabins. A man's body in a cycling position can have about four times the drag of a streamlined fairing large enough to encase him. In addition to the fuselage drag there is a further type of drag generated by the wing which is called 'induced' drag.

It will be remembered that in order for the wing section to produce lift there is a high pressure region under the wing and a low pressure region above. At the wing tip there is nothing to keep these regions apart and so the high pressure air flows over the wing tip into the upper region causing a

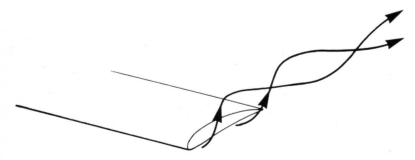

*Figure 11.* Development of a wing tip vortex.

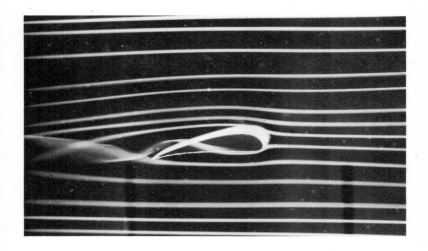

Smoke tunnel demonstration of both the development of the wing tip vortex and its reduction with decreased altitude. *Author's collection*

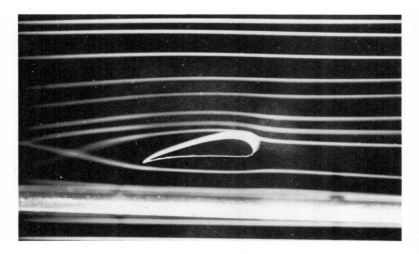

general movement of the air that shows as a vortex following the wing tip, illustrated in Figure 11. The air takes energy from the wing in order to produce the wing tip vortex and this shows up as an additional type of drag, which is the induced drag.

Now the induced drag can be a major proportion of the total drag of the aircraft. The actual magnitude of the induced drag depends upon the lift produced because this affects the creation of the high and low pressure regions below and above the wing which originate the wing tip vortex. Furthermore, the span of the wing has considerable effect because a long wing would be less influenced by its wing tip vortex behaviour than a short wing. Taking three man-powered aircraft and assuming that they are flying well away from the ground it is possible to estimate the relative magnitudes of the various drag percentages:-

|  | Malliga | Puffin I | Dumbo |
|---|---|---|---|
| Wing span | 64 ft. | 84 ft. | 120 ft. |
| Wing drag | 36% | 40% | 48% |
| Fuselage drag | 14% | 17% | 14% |
| Induced drag | 50% | 43% | 38% |

These three aircraft were chosen as the lifts derived from their respective wing sections were comparable and because they represent the present size range of man-powered aircraft. It is particularly noticeable that a major proportion of the total drag comes from the induced drag and that by increasing the wing span this can be reduced to some extent. However, this is not the complete picture as it was stressed that these values were for the three respective aircraft flying well away from the ground. When an aircraft is flying close to the ground, say with an altitude of 10 ft. or less, the proximity of the ground modifies the formation of the wing tip vortices and thereby reduces the induced drag. Therefore in practice, due to this 'ground effect', the magnitudes of the induced drag quoted would be reduced by about one third.

This ground effect was investigated after several low level crashes during the last war. These resulted when a heavily loaded plane just had enough power to take-off, the induced drag being reduced near the ground, but had insufficient power to climb and eventually crashed into low level obstacles.

Nevertheless, even with the benefit of the ground effect, the induced drag still forms a major proportion of the total drag of a man-powered aircraft. With a monoplane, and all the aircraft described in Chapter 3 come under this description, there are two wing tips from which the vortices develop. The chief reasons for biplanes being unpopular as man-powered aircraft, is that their total drag is very much greater than that of a monoplane. With a biplane there are four wing tips from which the vortices develop and therefore the induced drag is very much greater.

Two biplane man-powered aircraft have been built. The first was the Smolkowsky biplane which was constructed in 1965 at the Southern Alberta Institute of Technology at Calgary in Canada. The only known dimensions are an assumed total flying weight of 250 lb. and a total wing area of over 300 sq. ft. It is estimated that the wing span was not much longer than 30 ft. which is far too small for true man-powered flight even if using the most effective wing section available, which was certainly not the case with this machine. Some attempt was made to reduce the induced drag by using wing tip plates. The biplane failed to leave the ground under man-power alone but made several towed flights without power until it was damaged and the project shelved.

The second was BURD, a biplane project at the Massachusettes Institute of Technology. This had a biplane canard configuration, that is tail first, with a crew of two. Based upon serious scientific reasons, the choice of biplane configuration rested on its improved manœuvrability with two wings of shorter span. The span was 60 ft. which is quite small compared to the original 123 ft. span of Toucan. BURD

115

The *Smolkowsky* biplane during initial towed trials at Calgary in Canada. *Author's collection*

made a short hop in the spring 1974, but unfortunately had to be partially rebuilt owing to structural failure.

The designers of BURD have illustrated one of the fascinations of man-powered aircraft design in that they have purposely chosen a high drag configuration with a supposedly reduced performance in order to gain manoeuvrability. If one goes to the other extreme one can design for maximum performance by reducing the pilot's power input to a minimum. The optimum design on this basis is an aircraft of ¼ mile wing span flying at 3 m.p.h. and therefore totally impractical. Design must be realistic which means that the designer must compromise between all his constraints.

All man-powered aircraft except for Toucan have been single seaters for essentially practical reasons. The two seater machine has been proposed several times for its inherent benefits of improved power continuity and the fact that it allows one crew member to concentrate on controlling the machine. Following these arguments several writers have suggested larger crews. In boating terms even the use of coxed eights has been suggested. Unfortunately in practice the crew is the largest weight item of a present-day man-powered aircraft and if this weight is increased the size of the aircraft must be increased also.

Figure 12 shows a comparison between one and two seater man-powered aircraft. The graphs presented are based upon an assumed fuselage and crew weights of 190 lb. for the single seater and 350 lb. for the two seater, and a wing weight that varies directly with the wing span. As the distance of the wing above the ground varies, the induced drag can therefore vary the power requirements, it is assumed that the aircraft described in Figure 12 are flying at a wing height of 10 ft. above the ground. It will be seen clearly that a two seater machine requires a much larger wing span than a single seater to give the same power requirements. Larger machines have associated problems of handling and control, together with increased construction time, required workshop facilities and cost.

Therefore the usual design choice has been the smallest aircraft that would comply with the required aims, and this has invariably meant the choice of a single seat layout.

If one thinks in terms of man-powered aircraft suitable for either a student project or for sports flying, the aim must be to reduce the size still further so that construction can be cut to a minimum. Taking ½ h.p. as being available for the power, a study of Figure 12 clearly indicates that a single seat machine can be designed well under 60 ft. span that would comply with this requirement. Such a machine would be more suited for simple sports flying than the present generation of man-powered aircraft.

The design of small compact man-powered aircraft has only been possible through the development of the improved wing sections shown in Figure 9. Still further improvement would allow better aircraft designs to be conceived in the

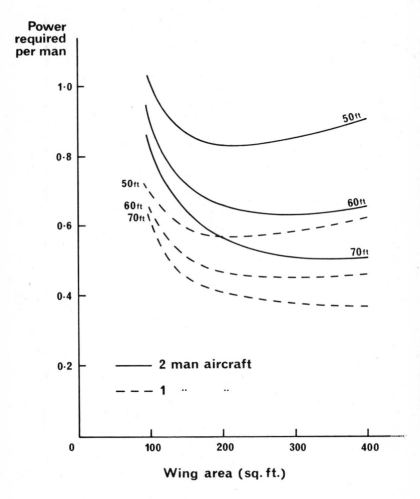

*Figure 12.* Comparison of one and two-seater man-powered aircraft.

future. As the development of wing sections for high performance gliders has largely stemmed from work carried out in German Universities the future development of man-powered flight could provide a link between practice and the fundamental research into low speed aerodynamics that is at present under way in some Universities and Polytechnics. Already theoretical studies have been performed that give hope of a new generation of wing sections with very high lift characteristics coupled with low drag. Whether these sections will demonstrate the same excellent performance in practice has still to be seen but certainly on the basis of the theoretical performance studies one can eventually hope for wing sections with working lift coefficients some 50% better than they are for the present-day Wortmann FX-63137 with the same high lift/drag ratio.

# 5

# Operational aspects

It is said that 'practice makes perfect' and this is as valid for man-powered flight as it is for any other physical activity requiring skill. However, from the number of flights quoted for particular man-powered aircraft in Chapter 3, it will be seen that most flight durations are only about a minute and that during this brief spell the pilot has to master both the control and propulsion of the machine. It is like an adult who has no previous cycling experience trying to master a bicycle in practice periods of one minute with occasionally months between practice periods.

This is why the performance set up by Jupiter is attributed more to the experience gained by the pilot, John Potter, than to any particular aerodynamic attributes of the aircraft. In no way is this meant to imply that the aerodynamic considerations are unimportant but that the developments outlined in the preceding chapters ensure aircraft designs having good performance capabilities. In order to realise those performance capabilities in practice there are operational difficulties to overcome, the greatest of which has been the lack of opportunities to acquire flight experience.

If we consider just man-powered flight since the first flight made by SUMPAC in 1961 and ignore those from towed launches, the total time in the air is still probably under 5 hours. Since this total flight time has been achieved during a period of well over a decade we are discussing in real terms man-powered flight durations totalling, on average, less than ½ hour per year. Coupled with the low flying time is the fact that it has been gained by 15 aircraft involving some twenty different pilots. It is therefore not surprising that man-powered flight has not progressed as rapidly as had been hoped and that no serious attempt has been made to gain the Kremer prizes.

As with all statistics one must not read too much into this value of 5 hours' flying time in man-powered flight. It highlights the problem but does not provide a complete picture of the whole situation. For example, although fifteen man-powered aircraft have flown, the major proportion of the total flying time has been amassed by three aircraft, Puffins I and II, and Jupiter. Furthermore, the flying of man-powered aircraft has not been consistent in each year, as most flying has been performed in the years 1962 and 1972. There is a sound reason for this; 1962 marked the testing of SUMPAC and Puffin I. Following the lessons learnt from the early flight trials it was indicated that more design improvements were required before performance could be improved. Many of the new generation of man-powered aircraft incorporating these improvements reached fruition in 1972 and so provided a total flying time of nearly one third of that accomplished in the whole of the preceding decade. There is sufficient information available on man-powered flight and sufficient aircraft already flying or in the process of being built to ensure that more should be achieved during the '70s than during the preceding decade.

However, the progress during the 60's in man-powered

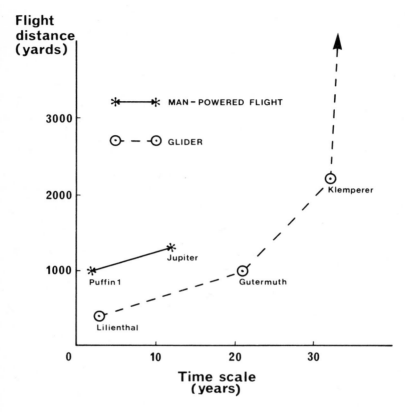

*Figure 13.* Comparison of the progress made in gliding and man-powered flight.

flight can be considered satisfactory when it is remembered that it is a pioneering activity. Figure 13 provides an interesting comparison between the progress in man-powered flight and that in gliding during its equivalent pioneering stage. Progress is portrayed in terms of significant flight distances on the vertical column and is plotted against a horizontal time scale of years. Although the time scale is the same for both man-powered flight and gliding, zero time is taken for the former as 1960 and for the latter as 1890.

It will be seen that when judged on this basis the progress in man-powered flight has been significant and provides a direct comparison with gliding during its first two pioneering decades. The development of man-powered flight is marked by two major performances, 993 yards achieved by Puffin I in 1962 and an unofficial 1,350 yards achieved by Jupiter in 1972. Development of gliding is marked by the best flight of Lilienthal in a hang-glider and by a flight of 1,000 yards made in 1911 by Hans Gutermuth. Subsequent progress in gliding was notably affected by the aeronautical development of the First World War and by the immense interest in gliding in Germany. The performance of Klemperer was that achieved at the 1921 Rhon meeting in his famous glider 'Blaue Maus'. The rapid improvement in performance thereafter can be attributed to the development of soaring techniques using hill lift and eventually leading to the use of thermals, so that by the end of the 20's glider flight distances were measured in tens of miles rather than in yards.

One must take care not to read too much into Figure 13 as the comparison is not strictly fair. All three glider performances noted were as the result of some loss of altitude down the sides of hills. Also it is difficult to find comparable pioneering eras in two activities, even though they represent the most closely related aspects of aeronautics. Nevertheless there are some significant points that do come out of this simple comparison. The first is that up to the Klemperer flight of 1921 the increase in numbers involved in gliding was sufficient to provide a real basis for improvement, either through direct competition or through communication of experience. Secondly the development of a new technique enabling performance to be extended by hill lift gave a vast improvement that was not necessarily related to any change in glider design. Subsequently gliders had to be modified so that they could manœuvre and be sufficiently strong to take advantage of the

123

lift in the atmosphere.

There is a third point which is a side issue, but nevertheless one of note. The progress in man-powered flight is represented in terms of the names of the aircraft whereas the early progress in gliders is represented by the names of the personalities involved. Of course in the early days of gliding the pioneers were brave in even attempting to fly because it was a new concept and one in which many enthusiasts did lose their lives. Certainly one does not want to see pilots killed attempting man-powered flight in order to boost the personality cult. It is indeed a very safe pursuit since the flying speeds are low and flights are carried out at low altitudes. However, the portrayal of man-powered flight in terms of aircraft is disturbing. Is it just a sign of the times or is the mass media concentrating too much attention on the design difficulties involved with man-powered aircraft?

Whatever the real answer is, there have been sufficient improvements in aircraft design to allow the development of man-powered aircraft with a range of operation potential. At one extreme there are man-powered aircraft with large wing spans needing low power input but needing large groups and facilities for their operation. At the other end of the scale there are small man-powered aircraft with a performance potential of 1—200 yards that are transportable, robust and capable of being flown in light winds. What is needed now is an increase in the man-powered flying time. This could not take place whilst some dramatic improvements in aircraft design were anticipated, but is now feasible.

If the rate of progress in man powered flight represented by the two points on Figure 13 is maintained, it will be the 1980's before we see the achievement of the magic one mile. On the other hand gliding illustrates the improvements that result from exploiting help from the atmosphere. If something similar could occur with man-powered flight — and this is discussed more fully in Chapter 7 in connection with sporting aspects — then it would be difficult to predict the achieve-

124

ments that could be made within a comparatively short time.

Before trying to look into the future it is well to assess the lessons learnt from past experience. In the particular case of man-powered flight this is made more difficult by the limited flying time and also because pilots have not recorded their experiences except for two notable exceptions, Derek Piggott's early flights with SUMPAC and the flying of Puffins I and II by three of the group's pilots.

Basically the problem with flying a man-powered aircraft is that the pilot has to fulfil the functions of both engine and controller. John Potter from his experience with Jupiter suggests that the pilot should train himself to operate his body in two completely separate modes. The lower half of the body is pedalling whilst the upper half controls.

In order to improve his power output John Potter ran up and down the runway in a tracksuit before each flight, getting himself thoroughly warm and putting himself in the right frame of mind. He was termed the 'hot' pilot, and warmed up whilst the aircraft was wheeled out of the hangar on to the runway with a second 'cold' pilot inside.

To train oneself to control requires the necessary experience and this can only be gained by actually flying. Jupiter has full controls which were fairly critical, especially the all-flying tail-plane, so that much of the pilot's attention had to be given to control. In fact with Jupiter flights had to be curtailed before maximum duration so that fatigue would not reduce the pilot's effectiveness to make fine control changes during landing.

The most important requirement for the pilot of a man-powered aircraft is the necessary power to get the machine into the air in the first place. Thereafter he should obviously have a clear understanding of how the machine will, or should, behave under flight conditions. Familiarisation with the controls is also essential as the pilot will rarely have sufficient time to think about their actual mode of operation whilst in flight. Since control of an aircraft by hands alone is unusual it is probably wise to relate the control mechanism to those with which the pilot has had previous experience. As a case in point the rudder control can be operated by means of a handlebar arrangement that can be directly related to steering a bicycle.

Puffin had the rudder operating by a handlebar which moved in the opposite direction of that of a bicycle. This was originally decided upon when the first pilot J. H. Philips decided it would be best to operate it in the direction of a conventional aircraft rudder bar. A later pilot, J. Wombwell, who made over thirty flights with Puffin II, admitted that he had difficulty adjusting to the direction of the control bar and that throughout his flying experience he still had to think occasionally for a few seconds about which way to make a turn. This was obviously not the ideal situation, particularly as in practice the rudder is the most important control.

From the pilot's point of view several layouts of the controls have been tried out in different man-powered aircraft. The simplest is that used for the Wright machine and Liverpuffin which just had rudder only control from handlebars. This relates most closely to bicycle practice, in fact one could say one was getting closer to the ideal of the bicycle of the air! As the pilots of the two aircraft were not trained to fly aircraft, the simplicity of control proved to be an effective arrangement in practice.

Other man-powered aircraft have had full controls for directional, lateral and longitudinal motions, usually by means of rudder, ailerons and elevator respectively. Exceptions have been Dumbo which had lateral control by means of variable wing angles of incidence, and Toucan which does not have a rudder but uses wing tip slot ailerons for directional control. Three basic types of cockpit layout for the control mechanisms have evolved and are shown in Figure 14.

The first, used on SUMPAC, employed a horizontal handlebar supported downwards from a vertical rod. Rudder was controlled by rotation of the handlebars, ailerons by moving

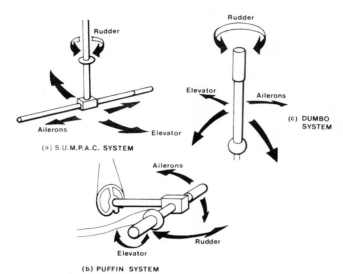

**Rudder**

**Elevator**

**Ailerons**

**Elevator**

**Ailerons**

(a) S.U.M.P.A.C. SYSTEM

**Rudder**

**Elevator**

**Ailerons**

(c) DUMBO
SYSTEM

**Ailerons**

**Elevator**

**Rudder**

(b) PUFFIN SYSTEM

*Figure 14.* Comparison of man-powered aircraft control system operations.

the controls from side to side and the elevator by moving forward or back. In principle this layout seems to be excellent as all the motions would appear to be the natural choice for each mode of control. However, in practice the friction in the control cables, together with the fact that the original rudder was too small, made the controls difficult to operate. Furthermore an all-flying tailplane was used for SUMPAC and such a form of longitudinal control is generally very critical in operation. It is not surprising that the pilot, Derek Piggott, described SUMPAC as being 'quite a handful'.

Puffins I and II, and also Jupiter, incorporated the second layout shown in Figure 14. This layout was designed for pilots operating from a cycling position and had a handlebar which was rotated for rudder control and rocked sideways for aileron control. Elevator control was by means of a twist grip on the handlebar. Apparently this system proved to be

127

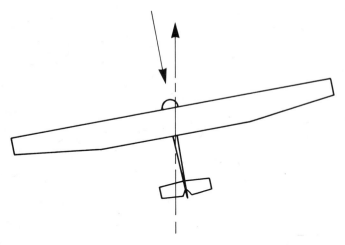

*Figure 15.* Yawing of man-powered aircraft in cross-wind, to maintain straight flight.

very satisfactory with the Puffin machines apart from the direction of rotation of the handlebars as already mentioned. Control of Jupiter was more critical, but this was more a problem of the aircraft design than of any inherent problem in the layout of the controls.

Jupiter incorporates an all-flying tailplane that is controlled by the twist grip mechanism and since this form of elevator control is critical anyway, it requires very precise control of the twist grip itself. Later flights were made with the aid of an instrument to provide an indication of the angle of incidence of the aircraft. In order to maintain the excellent flying performance of Jupiter the control in the air had to be precise, particularly to maintain a constant altitude. Perhaps the most tricky exercise with Jupiter was that of landing in a crosswind condition.

When flying with a crosswind the aircraft has to be yawed into the wind direction as illustrated in Figure 15 otherwise it would get blown off course. When flying in a straight line with Jupiter in such a crosswind the landing has to be assessed to within a few inches. Just before touchdown the rudder is used to turn the aircraft straight on course again otherwise the undercarriage wheel used for Jupiter buckles under the side loads. If the rudder is applied too early the aircraft straightens up on course but then has time to drift sideways which also tends to buckle the wheel. This wheel buckling problem is one that is particularly applicable to Jupiter owing to the type of wheel used and the very high loads. However, such a problem has also been experienced with the Malliga aircraft. Use of a slightly heavier but more robust undercarriage wheel that can take side loads is advisable.

The third form of control layout shown in Figure 14 is ideally suited to aircraft with the pilots in a reclining position. Control is basically by a stick as in a conventional aircraft, with forward and backwards movement for elevator control and side to side for lateral control. As this system was used for Dumbo the lateral control mode operated the centre structural mechanism of the wing to enable the two wing halves to change angle of incidence. This system has also been used for the Malliga aircraft, in which case the lateral control was in the form of transverse wing tip ailerons. In practice this type of control system has apparently been very satisfactory, particularly for pilots with previous flying experience as they can relate the movements for lateral and longitudinal control to those of a conventional aircraft control stick. Again the pilots apparently do not have difficulty in pedalling from a reclining position with the control stick between their legs. However, there must be some difficulty in operating the twist grip rudder control and a modification to incorporate a handlebar arrangement on top of the control stick might prove advantageous.

Although the three main types of control layout are shown in Figure 14 there are many other arrangements that could be used. For example the controls for Linnet II consisted of a handlebar with two twist grip controls, one for the elevator

129

the other for the rudder, whilst the ailerons were controlled by means of rotation of the handlebar. Such a system would appear to be difficult to co-ordinate in practice and has no apparent advantage over the three types of control systems discussed.

Turning from the control aspects to the actual flying of man-powered aircraft, the problems involved fall into two groups, one concerned with the part of flying that takes place along the ground during the take-off run and the other with the part of flying that takes place in the air. Dealing with the take-off run first, the problem is one of starting the aircraft from rest and accelerating the aircraft along the ground until it has reached a sufficient speed to take-off using man-power alone. In theory the power required to take-off should be no greater, and generally less, than that required for flight, as the aircraft is nearer the ground and the induced drag from the wing tip vortices is greatly reduced. In practice this seems to be the case, as most pilots of man-powered aircraft give the impression that take-offs were comparatively easy provided that they were from smooth runways. As soon as one attempts to take-off from a rough surface, say a tarmac runway with the surface breaking up or from short grass, the power required for take-off can double. It is impossible to attempt a man-powered flight from anything other than a runway with a reasonably good surface.

This unfortunately constitutes one of the major disadvantages of man-powered flight at the present time — the need to have ready access to an airfield with runway facilities. Things are getting better in this direction as the new generation of smaller man-powered aircraft can be flown in reasonably windy conditions of, say, 5 knots and need comparatively short take-off runs of 100 yards or less. This is a great improvement over past man-powered aircraft as Puffin I could not even be taken out of the hangar unless the wind speed was less than 6 knots. Puffin II, having an even larger wing span, was operated in lower wind speeds and actual flights were

130

John Potter at the controls of *Jupiter*, demonstrating the cycling position incorporated in this machine. *Crown*

made in winds of no greater than 2 - 3 knots.

Although a shorter take-off run would give a wider choice of airfields, the development of man-powered flight as a sport requires that there should be even more freedom of choice. It might be necessary to compromise between man-powered flight and gliding, and use some form of aid during take-off either in the form of a tow, catapault launch or power storage device.

Whatever future developments are made the present state of the art of man-powered flight has resulted from take-offs from reasonably smooth runways. In this case the power requirements for the take-off have been lower than for flights. Certainly from the author's personal experience with Liverpuffin the take-off seemed to be comparatively easy. The most difficult part was getting the aircraft to start moving in the first place. Once the aircraft was moving the pedalling

131

seemed to get progressively easier throughout the take-off run. Obviously not all aircraft can be the same, as John Potter recorded his experiences with Jupiter and stated that normally the tail lifted off at about 16 knots and from then on the acceleration up to the take-off speed of 18 knots represented hard work. This could be explained by the proximity of the ground having a less marked effect on the reduction of induced drag with Jupiter.

During the take-off run the aircraft must be stable, and this means having helpers steady the wing tips during the early part of the run. With aircraft equipped with lateral control they tend to become effective early in the run. For example with Puffin I the ailerons became effective at about 4 knots and in the case of Jupiter 5 knots. On the other hand the rudder did not become effective with Jupiter before about 8 knots. The helpers should therefore stay with the aircraft until it has reached their maximum comfortable running speed, say 8 - 9 knots, just guiding the wings but in no way holding them back, otherwise it will have a noticeable effect on the pilot's power requirements. At about this speed with man-powered aircraft the natural aerodynamic forces are generally greater than those that can be applied by the helpers anyway.

From then on during the remainder of the take-off run the pilot is on his own and can keep the aircraft straight along the runway by means of the rudder and, if the aircraft is so equipped, level by means of the lateral controls. The Wright aircraft and Liverpuffin have flown without the aid of lateral controls so that experiences gained from these aircraft are of value. The Wright aircraft has been flown only in very light wind conditions and so having a tricycle undercarriage remained level throughout the take-off runs, directional control being maintained by means of the rudder.

On the other hand Liverpuffin took off into a cross-wind and having one undercarriage wheel plus a tailwheel, was free to tip over. The take-off runs started with two handlers on

*Liverpuffin* during taxi-ing trial showing the heeling action caused by the side wind component. *Liverpool Echo*

the wings to keep them level but as soon as they let go the wings started to tip. From experience, as soon as the pilot feels himself tipping over there is an automatic reaction to stop pedalling. However, once one can steel oneself to ignore this reaction, the wings simply tip over until they reach a new stable position where the effect of dihedral can counteract the cross-wind component. In practice the pilot was only at some $5 - 6°$ to the vertical but even such a small angle can give a sense of insecurity until logic prevails and persuades one otherwise.

Difficulty can be experienced at the point of take-off owing to the miss-matching of the undercarriage and pro-peller if both are driven. Taking the simpler case of having just a driven propeller, the pilot can automatically adjust the rate of pedalling to provide the necessary thrust during the take-off run and through to flight. It is difficult to judge on the basis of available evidence whether it is better to have both driven undercarriage and propeller, or just propeller. Certainly the Linnet aircraft, Reluctant Phoenix and the Malliga aircraft have proved that it is possible to take-off with propeller thrust alone. However, their performances have been generally worse than those of man-powered aircraft with driven undercarriage, giving some slight indication that power requirements are greater when using propeller alone. However, the take-off run lengths for the Linnets and the Malliga machine are comparable with those of other man-powered aircraft. In the case of the Malliga machine the small propeller used had a much lower potential efficiency than those propellers used for, say, SUMPAC or Puffin I or II.

If a driven undercarriage and propeller are used they must be geared together. Take the hypothetical case of an aircraft having a flying speed of 20 m.p.h., having the wheel and propeller driven and the propeller adjusted to give the correct thrust when the wheel is turning at a speed equivalent to 20 m.p.h. With such an aircraft taking off in still air conditions, the propeller will provide the necessary thrust as soon as the wheel leaves the ground. However, supposing that the aircraft takes off into a 4 m.p.h. wind, the aircraft will leave the runway at a ground speed of 16 m.p.h. and the propeller will only be turning at $16/20$ of its correct speed. In this case the propeller will not be producing sufficient thrust to sustain flight but the aircraft will wish to leave the ground and the result is 'wheel slip'. This phenomenon has been experienced with SUMPAC, Puffin I and II, Liverpuffin, Toucan and, on at least one flight, with Jupiter.

Wheel slip, described most aptly by Derek Piggott as giving the feeling of cycling on patches of ice, is certainly a source of trouble particularly if one has to fly in light winds. A solution used for the first flight of Dumbo was to use the undercarriage for the early part of the take-off run then tip the nose up by means of the elevator and accelerate up to flying speed on propeller thrust alone. Alternatively a technique that was used with Puffins I and II was to hold the aircraft down on the runway until the speed was above that required for take-off. The excess speed gave the aircraft an impetus that enabled it to climb to a suitable altitude of a few feet during which time the pilot could modify his pedalling rate to the requirements of the propeller. However this technique requires some knowledge of one's speed, and for this several simple air speed indicators have been developed.

The simplest form of air speed indicator is the audible type suggested by Miller for hang-gliders, where a Cello pitch pipe is placed in the direction of the air flow and resulting notes give an indication of the speed. Figure 16 shows three other types of indicator. The flat plate (a) is hinged on an axis normal to the airflow and is deflected back by the air pressure on it. Either sheet aluminium or plywood can be used for the plate and the indication is given by noting the deflection of the plate or by means of a pointer and a scale as shown. This type of indicator was used on the Puffins and was mounted on an arm in front of the aircraft. Direct indication of speed was achieved by marking sections of the scale in different colours, red for stalling speed, yellow for cruising speed and green for above cruising speed.

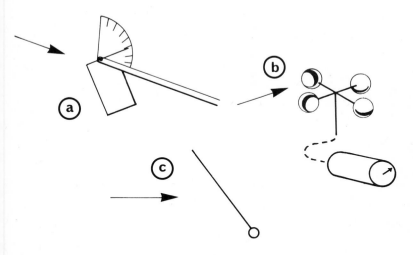

*Figure 16.* Various forms of air-speed indicator.

Malliga built a simple form of cup anemometer (b) in which he used four half table tennis balls and coupled it to a Volkswagen speedometer. This was used with some success on his aircraft except that it was originally mounted on top of the fuselage, which in a climb tended to blanket the air-flow to the anemometer. The last type of airspeed indicator (c) is also based on a table tennis ball; the ball is suspended from a thread and moves backwards because of drag created by the air flow. Although this type has not been used for man-powered aircraft it does seem to give a positive in-dication by means of the angle taken by the thread. Maximum speed with this indicator is of the order of 23 - 24 m.p.h. when the ball and thread are streaming out horizontally.

Once the take-off problems have been overcome the pilot's next task is to control the aircraft in the air whilst continuing to provide the necessary power. The limited flight experience with man-powered aircraft has meant that the majority of flights have been straight along the runway. Turns of up to 80° were attempted with SUMPAC with the turning require-ments of the 'figure-of-eight' Kremer course in mind. Gentle weaving on either side of the runway was carried out with Puffin I in order to gain experience of very gentle turns through small angles and this led to the performance defined for the 'slalom' Kremer course.

In order to extend flight lengths and reduce the power required from the pilot so that he could devote more atten-tion to control, two techniques were attempted by the Hatfield group with Puffin I. The first was to tow the aircraft behind a car, but this was discontinued as the aircraft got into an uncontrollable rolling oscillation, rolling from one side of the runway to the other in what was rather like a 'Dutch roll'. This is a term that describes a combination of both rolling and yawing and derives its name from the ice-skating on the canals of Holland.

The difficulty experienced when towing Puffin I could be partly explained by the flight taking place on a foggy day which meant the pilot did not have the horizon as a reference. Malliga has towed his man-powered aircraft several times and indicates that it is a very satisfactory method of allowing the pilot to gain initial control experience. The Hatfield group, after experience with Puffin I, decided to fit a model aero engine of 8 c.c. capacity that was found to provide most of the power required so that the pilot could put most of his effort into control.

Use of a model aero engine was apparently not always a blessing. It invariably started first flick whilst in the hangar but took up to 5 minutes to start on the runway, with the pilot becoming more uncomfortable as the time passed. With the aid of the engine John Wimpenny managed to do a 270° turn, with a reverse turn of 90° to land back on the runway again but facing in the opposite direction to the take-off run. Following this he expressed the view that 'the turn is not the big bogey that it is often thought to be'. Nevertheless man-powered flying has since concentrated on straight flights, as turns are hazardous with large wing span machines at low altitudes, and it has been found to be sufficiently difficult to extend flights in a straight direction.

The first impression in man-powered flight is the feeling one gets of actually leaving the ground. It is flying in the old-fashioned sense, which is most aptly described as 'flying by the seat of one's trousers', taken to an even finer stage because the moment the wheel leaves the ground the pilot experiences the direct sensation of lift-off. The other associated impression, at least for aircraft with the pilot in a cycling position in the nose, is the feeling of being much higher off the ground than one is. This feeling was described most effectively by J. Wombwell regarding his first flight with Puffin II. He held the nose down during take-off so that it was possible to build up speed, then twisted on the up-elevator and felt himself really soaring away. However on landing he found that he had only achieved an altitude of a foot. It is therefore difficult to judge one's height under such circumstances.

This is made worse by not having a lightweight accurate height indicator available, particularly for any attempt at the Kremer courses where one has to enter the course at a height of 10 ft. The Hatfield group progressed with Puffin II to the stage of making a trial attempt at the first leg of the simpler 'slalom' Kremer course. They used poles at the side of the runway from which the pilot could assess his height. Came the day of the first real trial on a calm day in August, 1967. John Wimpenny relates that he thinks it was about lunch time on a hot day, which was not ideal as the heat makes the pilot feel less energetic. To offset this effect is the possible benefit of rising air from the runway. After take-off and the climb to height he found the power requirements far greater than he expected on the basis of previous flight trials. He had to land shortly afterwards without attempting the course and found that one wing tip had been broken in striking one of the height indication poles.

Flying a man-powered aircraft along a straight course requires directional control as any slight gusts would throw the aircraft off course. During early flight trials with Puffin II it was found that the increase of wing span from the 84 ft. of Puffin I to 93 ft. gave a severe directional control problem. Any attempt to use both rudder and ailerons together resulted in a combined yawing rolling action, again similar to a Dutch roll. This was at last countered by developing a technique whereby the directional control was by means of the rudder alone and this technique has subsequently been employed for both Dumbo and Jupiter with success. Presumably for extended turns some form of controlled banking is necessary by means of lateral controls but for straight flights rudder control appears to be adequate.

Longitudinal control is normally exercised by means of the elevator and for flights near the ground is basically a 'fine' control in order to establish the correct angle of attack of the wing. With the limited power that is available for man-

*Figure 17.* Aircraft experiencing phugoid motion.

powered aircraft climbing can be achieved only by the pilot pedalling harder, or alternatively by outside help from the atmosphere, so that no elevator control is required. However, elevator control is useful when preventing a stall, although a well defined stall is not possible for man-powered aircraft only a few feet above the ground. Philips experienced a loss of lift with Puffin I whilst at an altitude of a few feet and found that the aircraft parachuted itself safely down to earth again. The most difficult part of longitudinal control of a man-powered aircraft is that of overcoming phugoid motion.

This is a state where the aircraft oscillates in an up and down motion as shown in Figure 17, and is basically due to the aircraft moving within a time period that is similar to the time required to operate the controls. Suppose the aircraft has the nose deflected up, the aircraft will climb and lose speed, by this time the pilot can operate the elevator to bring the nose down and the aircraft dives. It gains speed and so can 'zoom' up into a climb again which is made worse by the pilot over-controlling when realising that the aircraft is nose down. This phugoid motion is really applicable only to man-powered aircraft, as the time period for each oscillation is under 4 seconds. With ordinary light aircraft the basic phugoid oscillation takes place over 12 seconds or more and so can be automatically counteracted by the pilot.

It is made worse in man-powered aircraft if the elevator control is critical, and was experienced with both SUMPAC and Jupiter since they have all-flying tailplanes. Phugoid motion was also occasionally experienced with Puffin I and occurred when the pilot was trying to maintain the horizon at a constant position. If he flew by his air speed indicator and maintained a constant speed the phugoid motion disappeared.

Before leaving this brief discussion of the operational aspects of man-powered flight it is necessary to mention the weather. The most important aspect is that of wind. Man-powered aircraft fly at low speeds between 16 and 20 m.p.h., so that the stalling speed will be even lower. It is therefore impossible to think of flying an aircraft in a wind of speed equal to or greater than the stalling speed. This basically limits operation to a Force 3 wind (8 - 12 m.p.h.) which in simple terms is a light wind that shows itself by just starting leaves to rustle and move. In reality the past man-powered aircraft operations have been limited to Force 1 or 2 winds because of the additional difficulty of handling the aircraft on the ground.

In order to attain low wind conditions many flights have been made near dusk when the wind drops or during calm anticyclonic conditions. There are several well known anticyclonic periods in Britain that certainly provide calm weather conditions but give rise to fogs, or during the winter, hoarfrost. Fog can prevent the pilot from getting his bearings from the horizon. Worse still, fog or hoar frost deposited on the wing surface can give an appreciable increase in drag and therefore in power.

With smaller man-powered aircraft that can be operated in Force 3 winds the weather problem becomes less severe as the chances to fly are half as many again. Flying man-powered aircraft, like most other outdoor activities, would then probably find its most serious problem to be that of avoiding the rain.

# 6

# *Man-powered aircraft as student projects*

There is a trend in schools and institutions of higher education to develop students' creative ability by having projects of a design-make-test form. These can partly be embodied within the academic curriculum but mainly rely on the use of students' 'free' time. Many have been represented by the mass media through 'young scientist' competitions. However, except for the Liverpuffin project in Britain, the Linnet project in Japan, and a biplane project at St. Gabriel High School in the United States, no real attempt has been made to make man-powered aircraft a student project.

This is unfortunate, especially as a man-powered flight activity has most of the basic requirements of motivating interest and of allowing participation in a new and exciting field of study. A man-powered aircraft would be well suited to be a schools' project because of the generally practical nature of the involvement with such an activity. Schools usually have readily available handicraft work-shops and sports fields, facilities that are vital to such a venture.

One possible reason that schools have not yet attempted the building of a man-powered aircraft is the apparent lack of information regarding man-powered flight in general and the design of man-powered aircraft in particular. However, it is hoped that this present volume will provide some relevant information for such projects. The design and construction of a man-powered aircraft is associated with full size aircraft activities and so some engineering must be involved.

Engineering-biased projects are not easily associated with school activities as engineering is not generally taught and the students cannot extend their academic knowledge into practice as they can for projects associated with Physics or Chemistry. This is again unfortunate, particularly as we live in a so called 'technological society' where we regularly use, or are confronted by, the results of engineering activities.

This represents another advantage of man-powered aircraft projects, the fact that they provide an excellent introduction to an engineering activity but do not require specialist knowledge on the part of the students. They can extend their previous knowledge gained from aeromodelling or cycling and build a man-powered aircraft using techniques learnt within the handicraft courses. Design of a man-powered aircraft can be performed at whatever level the group wishes. The group must make design choices regarding the configuration and aerofoil section. These can be made realistically on the basis of previous experience with the man-powered aircraft listed in Chapter 3. Josef Malliga has amply demonstrated that an ad-hoc approach can result in a successful aircraft. The choice of construction can be made to suit the particular skills of the group or material availability. For a group with some theoretical knowledge at sixth-form or more advanced level a study can be performed from 'square one' using the basic aerodynamic design equations. Whichever design is chosen it is wise to make one's performance aims modest. Since nobody has yet won the Kremer prize it is impossible to say what sort of machine would be required with such performance aims in

143

mind. Judging from present experience the Kremer prizes will be won by fairly sophisticated aircraft, the term being used in a design sense. Such aircraft would be unsuitable for construction by groups as student projects.

It is therefore better to aim for a quite modest performance initially so that the resulting man-powered aircraft can be compact. This would enable the aircraft to have a relatively short wing span making it easier to construct, transport and handle. Judged from Figure 11 the order of wing span that is likely to be the most practical appears to be well below 60 ft. and if a lightweight pilot weighing less than 10 stone could be chosen, the wing span could be reduced below 50 ft. with every certainty of success. Such a wing span together with suitable choices of other geometric constraints, would ensure that the aircraft would be capable of man-powered flights yet still be small enough to comply with the other practical constraints.

Liverpuffin was the result of a University project and its wing span was chosen on the basis of similar practical considerations. The choice of the Liverpuffin project is instructive as the reasons for its choice are still partially valid for other types of academic establishment.

This project was part of the undergraduate course in engineering design at Liverpool University. Design can be considered to be that aspect of engineering that actually defines an end result, the end result usually being in the form of hardware. The actual hardware MUST work and this is the basic requirement of any design. It is no use having beautiful and creative ideas if they cannot be translated into practice. In order for the undergraduates to gain experience of design under 'real' constraints several small projects had been introduced of a design-build-test nature. For example they made a 'paper bridge' — a structure to span 2 ft. with a central load of 10 lb. built of drawing paper and adhesive tape and to have minimum weight. There was also a 'soft-landing device' — a simple and cheap device to prevent an egg from being broken

144

when dropped from a height of 8 ft.

These simple projects allowed the students to judge their original design ideas by their success, or otherwise, at the testing stage. However these projects were considered to be unrealistic for undergraduates going through specific training for a future career in engineering. In practice a designer would have to tackle complex problems involving many different aspects of design. As an experiment it was therefore decided to base a one year undergraduate design course on one major project. The particular year chosen was the intermediate one of the three-year course and the students would therefore have some basic knowledge of design from their initial year of study. A further important fact was that a workshop measuring 30 ft. x 18 ft. had been opened solely for the use of undergraduates working on design projects.

It is difficult in retrospect to decide which came first, the decision to make a man-powered aircraft and to organise the project accordingly, or the realisation that, having assessed the aims of the project, the man-powered aircraft was the obvious choice. Whichever way it developed, the reasons for the design and construction of a man-powered aircraft being chosen can be summarised as follows:-

1. The complexity of the design and the required organisation should be comparable with projects found in industry.

2. The theoretical design would give the students experience with the application of their basic knowledge whilst the actual aircraft could be built with the limited skills and tools available to the students.

3. There was, and still is, no standard solution to the design of a man powered aircraft so it was argued that the students would have to use their initiative and could not simply copy existing designs.

In view of these pertinent reasons the man-powered aircraft went ahead even though counterclaims were made for a medical-engineering project. Furthermore, as neither of the

145

lecturers involved had specialised aerodynamic training, doubts were raised as to the ultimate success of the project. It was argued in favour of the man-powered project that specialised knowledge can be as much a disadvantage as an asset. What was needed for success was a balanced approach, taking into account structural and practical constructional criteria as well as the aerodynamic requirements. Also if the lecturers themselves had to tackle new problems in aircraft design they would appreciate the students' problems more readily and, it was hoped, the students would learn by direct observation of the lecturers' approach to new problems.

At the start of the project information was available on three previous British man-powered aircraft, SUMPAC, Puffin I and Puffin II, the information being in the form of articles in periodicals and a cine film of flights made by SUMPAC and Puffin I. Thus the students started with more knowledge of the experience gained that had been available to many designers of man-powered aircraft. The publication of this book since the start of the Liverpuffin project ensures that new man-powered aircraft projects can now be started with a better insight into previous developments.

The Hatfield group heard about the project and, having the crashed remains of Puffin II, offered these as a basis for the new aircraft. Parts from the crashed Puffin II were received in September 1969 and those that were useable included the pilot support frame, propeller, primary wing structure after being repaired, and the tail surfaces again after being repaired. Although on balance their acquisition was advantageous there were disadvantages. For instance a great deal of time and also money had gone into Puffin II so the construction tended to be elaborate and of excellent workmanship. Obviously the engineers at de Havilland had treated this project in a similar way to that of a full size aircraft. The students had a sense of inferiority because they realised they could not achieve the same level of manufacture. The other disadvantage was that having the primary wing structure and pilot support frame

146

did restrict the freedom of the undergraduate design.

An important factor that had to be fully appreciated was that Puffin was designed and built having large workshop/ hangar facilities. Puffin could be fully assembled in the hangar than simply wheeled out for each particular flight. The Liverpool aircraft on the other hand would need to be designed for construction in our comparatively small work-shop then transported 24 miles to a local airfield for flight trials.

Unless one is offered a complete man-powered aircraft that requires only a small amount of repair work before it can be flown, it is much better to start such a project from scratch, particularly in view of the enthusiasm that should be generated by a complete project.

Projects have elements of 'fun' and also elements of work within them. Clearly for anyone to get involved in such a project the 'fun' element must be sufficiently attractive to make the work worthwhile. This is a truism as it applies to any activity, but it is a feature of basic motivation that must be allowed for. One section that can be 'fun' is the choosing of the particular configuration and parameters for the air-craft, even if in the end it comes back to the choice of an existing design. At least it is a choice that can be made freely and in which the group's members can participate. Other 'fun' areas are the satisfaction derived from actually constructing something and from the ultimate thrill of seeing the machine take to the air.

Organisation of the particular Liverpuffin project represen-ted a difficulty that was never really solved. Two lecturers organised the project on which 74 students worked during the academic year. In view of this extremely large ratio of students to staff it was decided, on the basis of previous experience with other projects and from similar organisational techniques employed in industry, to split the students into groups of six with a student group leader in charge of each. In this way it was hoped that the lecturers would have direct

147

contact with the group leaders and the responsibility would be delegated to each student in the only practical manner available. Organisation was made more difficult by having only two hours' direct contact between lecturers and students allocated each week on the time-table.

Although the ideal situation would have been for each student to look at each aspect of the design project this was unrealistic. Division of the design into particular aspects of the project, first to the group, and then by further sub-division of work to each student in the group, was necessary. This method of working had the advantage of allowing students to appreciate how such projects are tackled in industry whilst still allowing direct communication with members of other groups in order to assess the overall design considerations.

Students entering the course did not have any prior knowledge of man-powered aircraft or, in most cases, of aerodynamics. The first term provided the students with sufficient knowledge of aerodynamics to check the power required for a particular configuration and to appreciate what effect changes in configuration would have.

The final weeks of the first term were spent in discussion assessing the findings of the various groups and using this to decide on the aircraft configuration. The findings of the students were summarised as:-

i.     That it was impractical at the present 'state-of-the-art' to aim at the Kremer Prize. This was largely based on the view that Puffin II was the most sophisticated man-powered aircraft to have flown, yet it had not complied with the requirements of the prize.

ii.    Because of the need for transportation, and to minimise repairs, the proposed man-powered aircraft would need to be robust.

iii.   In order to accommodate a wide variety of possible student pilots the input power should not be greater than ½ h.p.

iv.    That help could be gained from convection up-currents provided that the aircraft could be flown on warm days during the afternoons.

v.  That in theory it was possible for the proposed aircraft to be designed with inherent lateral stability. Although this would probably cause the aircraft to 'wallow' in flight it was considered to be acceptable as elimination of lateral control would greatly simplify the pilot control problem. Turns would still be possible using rudder alone although manœuvrability was not considered to be of primary concern.

On their own the students were quite happy to discuss these findings in general terms but were not prepared to use them as a basis for decisions regarding the aircraft configuration. This was mainly due to having a large group of undergraduates with so many different opinions. The lecturers finally had to channel these opinions and findings into one direction and the final configuration chosen was that shown in Figure 18. A high wing, chosen for stability, with a functional pod-and-boom fuselage providing a large moment arm for the rudder and tailplane, and a short drive length from pilot to the propeller. Wing span was originally chosen as 68 ft. but was later reduced to 64 ft. in a fairly arbitrary manner when information regarding the success of the Malliga aircraft came to hand.

It was appreciated that the construction would be the most difficult stage of the project so at the beginning of the second term the whole group of students was allowed to decide democratically whether they wished to proceed with the man-powered aircraft project. It was pointed out that the detail design and construction stages represented the most difficult parts of the project and that if they thought it was too ambitious the emphasis could be changed to teaching design through shorter projects, as in the previous year. The group voted to continue with the major project.

It was difficult during the detail design stage to persuade students to make the transition from innovation to detail.

149

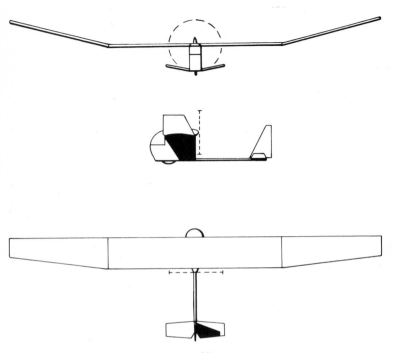

*Figure 18*. Configuration of *Liverpuffin*.

All too often during the first few weeks of the second term a group of students would come forward with an idea for a design but without any details or anything on paper. When told to quantify their idea they would go away only to change the idea for something 'better' and later present this, again without anything on paper. Even when initial design proposals were committed to paper and were accepted the students still tended to change their minds as new ideas came along.

Although the importance of time was stressed, the problem of getting students from the innovation stage to that of constructing from a detailed design was never fully solved. This was entirely due to the large number of students that each lecturer had to deal with during each class. If the lecturer could have spent say a minimum of 20 minutes with each student each week then this problem would not have occurred to the same extent. One must always accept that there will be some poorly motivated students who prefer to just 'think' about the problem rather than carry out the necessary but probably tedious design work.

Because of these problems the detailed design stage took far longer than was originally expected or intended. The two lecturers continued to direct students towards making the necessary decisions themselves because it was always borne in mind that the project was basically a teaching aid rather than the building of a man-powered aircraft. Nevertheless by the end of the second term many of the design detail problems had been solved and some construction started, but in some cases this was only achieved by the lecturers forcing the students in the right direction.

The most ingenious item of design was the secondary structure of the wing. Previous man-powered aircraft had used

View of *Liverpuffin* clearly showing the pod and boom form of the fuselage and the different constructional techniques used for the wing. *Liverpool Echo*

ribs built from strip balsa which, although satisfactory, were fragile and warped with changes in humidity. The main criterion for the secondary structure was low weight, which directed the students' attention to expanded polystyrene (E.P.S.). The other criterion of importance to the students particularly was ease of construction, and they decided that wire-cutting E.P.S. would be easier and quicker than building up a large number of separate ribs. In retrospect this conclusion is invalid but at the time it appeared to be the best solution and provided a more robust structure. A piece of angle iron was accidently dropped on the leading edge. With a balsa structure this would have necessitated a partial re-build but with E.P.S. all that resulted was a small dent.

The form of the E.P.S. structure was of longitudinal hollow sections with thin transverse sheets of E.P.S. to increase the torsional stiffness. Circular lightening holes were added to minimise weight. E.P.S. of under 1 lb./cu. ft. density was used throughout for the secondary structure, apart from the trailing edge where stronger E.P.S. of nearly 2 lb./cu. ft. density was used because of the thin sections involved.

It had originally been proposed to use E.P.S. for the whole of the wing secondary structure but in practice it was applied only to the constant chord centre wing panel. Because of the taper on the outer wing panels the use of E.P.S. would have required the construction of a large number of templates before cutting the foam to shape with hot wire, so the design was modified to the use of sheet balsa ribs. A balsa sheet thickness of 3/16" was employed for the ribs and as the total weight of each of the 17 ft. long outer wing panels was only 15 lb. its use, compared to built up strip balsa ribs, did not add appreciably to the overall weight, yet provided a more robust structure. However, care was taken to choose balsa sheet of the minimum density available.

Throughout the final stages of the one-year major project the construction of the aircraft proceeded to the stage where most of the centre panel of the wing and the basic structure

152

of the fuselage were completed. Subsequent construction was continued by staff and as a result of small student group projects until the aircraft was completed in December 1971, a matter of some two and a quarter years from the start of the project. In spite of problems of organisation and the student motivation involved in the major one year project, the comparatively short time between the start and the completion of the aircraft was a genuine source of satisfaction, and confirmed the original view that the construction of a man-powered aircraft was practicable.

Looking at the Liverpuffin project in retrospect and trying to draw general conclusions, it is evident that a man-powered aircraft makes an excellent student project. Although there were organisational problems with the Liverpuffin project these would have occurred in such a large group with any other project. The major difficulty arose in persuading the students to define their ideas, especially when moving from the creative stage to that of detail design and construction.

This is a problem of discipline and one that cannot be solved with large student/staff ratios. It must be assumed that at the undergraduate level students will not allow themselves to get too deeply involved in design projects because they are more concerned with examination results. With large groups it is possible to discipline students only by imposing a strict time schedule. Human nature being what it is, most students tend to leave things till the last moment and this must be combated during a design course by requiring completion of specific pieces of work at regular intervals during the academic year. Unfortunately this technique does not necessarily fit in with the requirements of a major project.

Outside the confines of such a highly concentrated academic course the choice of a man-powered aircraft as a student project is an attractive one. From an organisational point of view it is feasible, and indeed more practicable, to approach the construction of such a machine with a small group of say up to a dozen students with a leader who takes charge of the

153

basic organisation. The group leader would probably be a staff member, but whoever it is his primary function is to maintain full communication with the group members to ensure that each is fulfilling a specified function within the required time period; also to ensure that each group member can contribute in the most effective way to the project by being able to feed back information to the leader and to other members of the group.

From a design point of view the choice of a man-powered aircraft for such a project should not be too ambitious. It is much better to be able to complete a simple, compact aircraft than to have a more complex one unfinished. However it must be borne in mind that eventually a pilot is going to be suspended in the machine at some height from the ground, even though it may be only a few feet, so the machine should be

Josef Malliga explaining the constructional use of foam plastic for the wing of his aircraft. *Josef Malliga*

not only simple but also robust. As a general design rule strength is more important than performance, as performance can be developed but something that is not strong enough will fail anyway. In the case of a man-powered aircraft if through making the machine adequately robust the weight increases to the point where actual man-powered flight is impossible then it can still be flown as a simple glider or with additional help from the use of model aeroengines.

An excellent example of a simple robust man-powered aircraft is the Malliga machine, a design that incidentally required the minimum of construction time. Construction of the wing is particularly interesting as the primary structure was of aluminium tubing tapering from 4" diameter at the centre down to about 1½" at the wing tips, with a secondary structure of E.P.S. ribs. The primary structure was originally too weak for extended flights at the comparatively high altitudes to which Malliga has towed the machine so that it was braced by tension wires from the undercarriage to the aluminium tubing at points several feet away from the fuselage. What is even more reassuring with regard to potential student projects is that the Malliga aircraft was completed by one person within a six month period.

# 7

# *Man - powered flight as a sport*

Any endeavour must have positive aims to warrant its continuing and those for man-powered flight up till now have been to prove the feasibility of such a form of aviation, to attempt to win one of the Kremer prizes or to provide the basis for a student project. The most powerful of these reasons has been the Kremer prizes and we have the competitions to thank for the incentive given to many of the developments of the past decade. However none of the machines so far built has complied with the requirements of the Kremer competitions.

There are several reasons for this, but the main one is the increase in power required for an aircraft to climb, for without this restriction it is likely that at least one aircraft, Puffin II, would have been entered for one of the Kremer competitions. Most man-powered aircraft would need to fly at an altitude of one or two feet for most of the course in order to take advantage of the reduction in induced drag due to the ground effect, then climb back to the 10 ft. altitude required at the finishing line. Power for climbing is greater than that for level flight and for any aircraft with an L/D ratio of 50, as achieved by the later man-powered aircraft, the power at a 1° climbing angle would be nearly twice that needed for cruising.

Such a climbing angle is very shallow, being roughly equivalent to a rise of 1 foot in a flight distance of 20 yards. In this respect the £5,000 Kremer competition in which the competitors have to complete two 'slalom' flights, could be more difficult in reality than the £50,000 Kremer competition which retained the initial 'figure of eight' course.

It must not be inferred from the foregoing remarks that the Kremer competitions are an impossible achievement, but there must be further developments before they can be won. The competitions themselves may not provide the necessary encouragement for such developments.

The problem is that all the aircraft have so far been designed for a direct attempt at the competition where the crew are required to provide all the power for the flight unaided by any help from the atmosphere. In order to extend flights the aim has been to reduce power input by increasing wing spans, resulting in machines that are subject to the following restrictions:-

i) Can be flown only in very calm conditions, either at dusk or early in the morning, so limiting flying experience.

ii) Can be entrusted only to expert pilots, so possibly limiting the power available for propulsion.

iii) Construction can be attempted only by large dedicated groups. In this respect it must be mentioned that the Weybridge aircraft initially involved 10,000 man hours of construction time and the Cranwell group spent a further 1,200 hours on reconstruction before it could be flown.

iv) Such machines require that large workshop/hangar and flying field facilities are *readily* available.

The last two restrictions obviously limit the number of

such aircraft that can be built and with the present restricted nature of the aircraft industry, future attempts at building aircraft of the size of Weybridge or Toucan cannot be envisaged.

At the present time we have the Weybridge and Toucan machines with wing spans of 120 and 139 ft. respectively. They are designed to fly around the complete course at an altitude of 10 ft. since the decrease in induced drag at lower altitudes is smaller. In the case of the Weybridge machine the power saved by reducing altitude from 10 to 3 ft. is only 5%, so in theory these aircraft can zoom to 10 ft altitude from an increased take-off speed and maintain altitude throughout the remainder of the course. However, in practice these large aircraft require light wind conditions in order to attempt flights and this will restrict the amount of flying that is necessary for the crew to gain experience in order to compete for the Kremer prize.

Bearing all this in mind it is considered that designing and constructing man-powered aircraft solely for a direct attempt at the Kremer competitions is an impractical exercise at the present time. To continue with this as the main aim of man-powered flight would limit developments since the machines required for such attempts require extensive facilities and a dedicated group who are prepared to spend several years on the construction. On the other hand to build more practical machines simply to continue to prove the feasibility of man-powered flight is unnecessary after the flights over the past decade. For any activity to develop there must be a positive aim and it is suggested that the future for man-powered flight must lie not only in its suitability for student projects but more generally in its development as a sporting activity, where competitions could provide the incentive for human interest and improvement in designs. In fact the two aspects of man-powered flight could be linked very effectively, with aircraft built as the result of student projects being used for sports flying just as gliders built by student groups in Germany have aided, and continue to aid, the development of soaring flight.

The suggested development of man-powered flight as a sport is based on the expected enthusiasm that would result from such an aim, and also on the past history of gliding which indicates that sporting competitions are powerful incentives to improvement of the performance of the aircraft themselves. Therefore the change in direction of man-powered flight towards being a sport could eventually lead to the winning of the Kremer prizes.

When compared with gliding the development of man-powered flight as a sport is a logical and possibly inevitable step, as any aeronautical activity that does not have a basically military application must decline unless given a civil purpose, which in this case can lie only in a sporting direction. Although one does not wish to look ahead too far the idea of man-powered flight pursued as a sport at just club level would be sufficient to ensure its continuance. However in practice man-powered flight should appeal to a wider range of people than any other aeronautical activity.

Gliding is restricted by the need for elaborate equipment to tow the machine into the air in the first place. This means that for every flight time must be spent in arranging the relevant equipment and that several people are involved with each launch in controlling the tow device, handling the tow cables on the ground, signalling and handling the actual glider. Man-powered flight basically relies on the pilot's energy to get himself airborne so that ideally a minimum of two people, the pilot and one handler, would be sufficient for each take-off. It is not meant to imply that gliding and man-powered flight are comparable at the present time and that because of the possible ease of launching man-powered flight has an obvious advantage, but it does give hope for the distant future when technology can provide machines that are sufficiently light and sufficiently strong to allow a combination of the merits of both types of flying.

At the present time man-powered aircraft are light and

home-built so that the first cost of each machine is far lower than for any other form of flying. Since man-powered flight is still at a pioneering stage it is not restricted by the rules and regulations that are necessary for more established activities, so that anyone can fly whether they have previous flying experience or not. From an aeronautical point of view, man-powered flight has many advantages. This is particularly true for aeromodellers who for the same cost as a large radio controlled model aircraft can build a man-powered aircraft in which they could fly themselves.

However, man-powered flight has not only aeronautical appeal but could develop as an athletic activity also. As our roads become more crowded and polluted so man-powered flight could provide a suitable outlet for cyclists. There must be many cyclists who, if given the opportunity, would willingly exchange the carbon monoxide and the inspiring view of cars and lorries passing them at close quarters for the wide open spaces at even a couple of feet above green fields.

One major advantage of man-powered flight at the present time is its safety. As all man-powered flights have taken place, and will continue to take place within the foreseeable future, at very low altitudes and low speeds the chances of serious injury are minimal. Other advantages are its silence and the fact that it does not pollute the atmosphere. The Liverpuffin whilst on display in the United States was heralded as the most pollution-free aircraft there. Since the Western World becomes increasingly more conscious of ecology this point is worth bearing in mind.

However, before man-powered flight can be developed as a sport, a more practical type of aircraft is required that ideally should embody the following attributes.

i) It should be simple and capable of being constructed by individuals or by small groups having limited workshop facilities.

ii) It can be transported easily to the flying field and rapidly assembled for flight.

iii) It must be capable of being flown in light wind conditions of say 10 knots, otherwise flying would be very restricted.

iv) It should be sufficiently robust to withstand such mishandling as would be inevitable during transportation and during training of the pilot.

All these requirements lead to the need for man-powered aircraft of minimum wing span compatible with the necessary low power input. The design of a small man-powered aircraft such as the 50 ft. wing span machine being developed by Tony Paxton should comply more closely with the requirements of a sporting machine than any others that have flown to date. This is a light-weight machine of only 85 lb. empty weight, that utilises the GU25 - 5 (11) 8 high lift aerofoil section. In order to carry out the initial trials the aircraft was towed behind a bicycle so that the development could proceed in a logical manner, first testing the aircraft before trying out the propeller and drive system. The initial towed trial failed to get the aircraft off the ground, showing the need for

Tony Paxton's compact man-powered aircraft during construction. *Author's collection*

161

subsequent developments that have since proved successful. Although not ideal, the construction of this type of machine can allow the development of man-powered flight as a sporting activity, thereby providing the knowledge for future design improvement.

During take-off the power requirements for this type of machine would be less than the ½ h.p. estimated for level flight cruising conditions because of the decrease in the induced drag, so that a fairly light man of 10½ stone or under and with average fitness could be sure of getting airborne and having short flights of 50 to 100 yards. Performance could be extended by the use of athletes as pilots and this would be an obvious requirement for competition at national level. Since such a machine should be far easier to manage than any of the man-powered aircraft that have previously flown it would be more practicable to have athletes as pilots.

There have been many suggestions for extending performance with non-athletes as pilots, including the use of power storage devices, buoyant gas in the wings and the utilisation of low altitude lift from the atmosphere. Dealing with the use of buoyant gas first, the problem is that there is insufficient volume within a man-powered aircraft to make it worthwhile unless one has an inflatable machine such as the Reluctant Phoenix. If one could fill the whole of a typical fixed wing it would provide only about 5 lb of lift and the complexity of ensuring that the wing was completely gas-tight could impose a weight penalty of more than 5 lb.

Regarding power storage devices, these can be either internal and carried within the aircraft or external to aid take-off. Although some ideas regarding the use of stretched rubber have been suggested, a successful power storage device has not yet been developed for use within a man-powered aircraft. Energy can be stored in accumulators of either electrical or fluid variety, by stretching springs or rubber and by means of rotating flywheels. The problem is to devise a power storage unit that is sufficiently light to be carried within a man-powered aircraft so that the power requirements are not greatly increased, yet capable of storing enough power to make a significant difference to the man-power requirements.

The use of external power devices to aid take-off would be particularly useful as they would allow greater freedom in the choice of fields for flying. In this respect the rubber 'bunjie' as used for both the Haessler-Villinger and Bossi-Bonomi machines represents the simplest form of launching device, although it places increased stress on the aircraft structure. Ideally a 'bunjie' launch can be carried out single handed. In the case of the Haessler-Villinger aircraft the pilot could anchor the machine to the ground then stretch out the rubber cords, anchor them to the ground and then release the aircraft from within the cockpit.

In reality the utilisation of atmospheric lift appears to be the most preferable method of increasing the performance during flight, especially as it would allow a much wider range of pilots to participate in sporting man-powered flight. With help from the atmosphere the main requirement is to get the aircraft to stagger into the air and then have the man-power in reserve when the lift fades away. However, man-powered flight would still be restricted to very low altitudes, at least within the foreseeable future, as the aircraft must be sufficiently light to allow flight by man's power, and this of necessity restricts the strength that would be required to combat the more turbulent air at higher altitudes. Once the development of sporting man-powered flight was established it can be envisaged that more robust designs could evolve making use of new materials such as carbon fibres, but at greatly increased cost.

Three types of atmospheric lift can be encountered at the low altitudes relevant to man-powered flight. If we think in terms of altitudes below 50 ft. the three types of lift are:-

1) Convection up-currents
2) Orographic lift
3) Dynamic lift

In theory even a small amount of help from the atmosphere should extend a man-powered flight. Considering a simple man-powered aircraft such as the Paxton machine of 50 ft. span, it has a lift-drag ratio of about 25 when operating near the ground so that if just gliding it would lose height at a rate of about 1 foot per second. In reality if the aircraft were just gliding with the propeller stationary the glide ratio would be worse than this due to the increased drag of the propeller, so it would be better to keep it turning. However to continue with the basic theme, if the aircraft entered a region of atmospheric lift where the air was rising at 1 ft./sec. then clearly it would maintain its height without any help from the pilot. With air rising at more than 1 ft./sec. the aircraft would gain height and equally obviously if the air were rising at less than 1 ft./sec. the aircraft would lose height without help from the pilot. With lift of only 1/3 ft./sec. the pilot would have to make up the equivalent of the other 2/3 ft./sec. in order to maintain height. Instead of the nominal ½ h.p. required for normal level flight, he would need to put in only two thirds of that power i.e. 0.33 h.p. and so would be able to pedal for a longer duration.

When a region of air is warmed with relation to the surrounding air, it rises and thereby creates a convection up-current. This process is taking place throughout the atmosphere and is the reason for the creation of thermals and the cumulus clouds that abound on warm sunny days. Briefly, if a bubble or column of warm air is rising from the earth's surface it is called a thermal. Although the warm air within the thermal will expand and cool as it gets higher, so long as it remains warmer than the surrounding air it will continue to rise. Since the air in the thermal contains water vapour it will eventually reach a height where the temperature is sufficiently low for the moisture to condense and form cumulus clouds.

Thermals are used by gliders but do not begin to develop in any well defined manner until several hundred feet up, well above the level at which they could benefit man-powered

164

flight. Therefore the type of convection up-current that we need for man-powered flight must not be confused with thermals at all. Unfortunately there is little information on low altitude convection currents simply because they have no real practical significance for other forms of aviation. Certainly they exist and on hot sunny days it is possible to see the warm air rising. Their creation depends on the amount of sunlight and the dampness of the surface together with its ability to absorb or reflect solar heat, since such up-currents can only develop over an area whose surface temperature is greater than those of the surrounding areas.

A runway, particularly one of black tarmacadam, will absorb more solar heat than the surrounding grass and so give rise to up-currents. In theory an up-current rising at 1 ft./sec. could be achieved at a height of 10 ft. above the runway with only $2°$ F ($1°$C) temperature difference between the runway and the surrounding grass. In order to take advantage of such up-currents it is necessary to fly on warm sunny days when automatically the presence of up-currents would create winds. Therefore it is possible to envisage small man-powered aircraft, that can be flown in reasonable wind conditions of say up to 10 knots, being able to take advantage of such up-currents. Such up-currents must be balanced by down draughts in adjacent regions. Thus the only means of assessing the use of convection up-currents is actually to attempt man-powered flights under such conditions and learn from direct experience.

It is difficult to envisage cross country flights based upon up-currents of this nature simply because of the uncertainty of their positions, so we are not able to foresee man-powered flight making quite the dramatic breakthrough that gliding did in the 1920's when flight distances increased in the space of a few years from one to tens of miles. Also the thought of cross-country trips at altitudes of below 50 feet leaves much to the imagination. Although one cannot envisage such types of flight, the use of up-currents could lead to developments that are as unforseen to us as cross-country flight measured

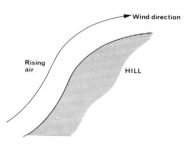

*Figure 19.* Diagram of the creation of orographic lift.

in hundreds of miles would have been to the early gliding pioneers.

Orographic lift is that created when a surface wind has to rise over a hill, as illustrated in Figure 19. This type of lift is widely used by glider pilots, who by tacking backwards and forwards over the crest of a hill remain within the region of maximum lift. Since in Britain the prevailing winds are from the West there are several gliding clubs that have well established hill-soaring sites on westerly facing slopes. An excellent example is that at Sutton Bank near Thirsk in Yorkshire, where the hill suddenly rises by some 500 feet from the relatively low lying plain to the West. The gliding site is obviously on top of the slope so that the gliders can be launched into the region of maximum lift.

Pilots have to know their sites very well because the lift is not consistent due to imperfections in the shape of the hill itself. The chances of using orographic lift for man-powered flight are uncertain. Clearly one cannot go launching such weak machines from the top of 500-foot-high hills, so that the height of the slopes or hills would have to be limited to probably a tenth of this to begin with. The area of lift developed by such a small slope would be limited and might be too small to accommodate a man-powered aircraft of even 50 ft. wing span, particularly if the usable wind speed was restricted to 10 knots.

166

A more directly useful type of lift would appear to be dynamic lift, at least during the initial development of man-powered flight as a sport. Dynamic lift depends upon the wind gradient near the surface of the ground. When meteorologists talk of a 10 knot wind they mean a wind that has a speed of 10 knots at a height of 33 ft. above the ground. Beneath that the wind will be slowed down by friction between the air and the ground so that actually on the surface of the ground the wind speed is zero. Most of the change in wind speed takes place within the first two or three feet but above this there is a steady increase of wind speed up to about 30 ft.

The effect of the wind gradient can be judged from a simple example. Supposing we have a man-powered aircraft flying

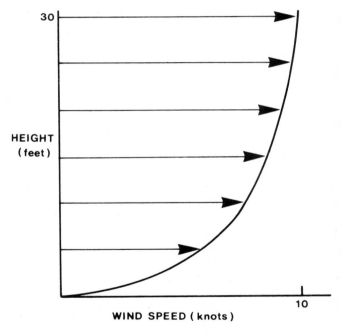

*Figure 20.* Variation of wind speed with height near the ground.

at an altitude of 5 ft at a steady speed of 15 knots in still air conditions. Now let us assume that a 10 knot gust of wind comes along. as illustrated in Figure 20 and meets the aircraft head on. At 5 ft. altitude the actual wind speed may be about 6 knots so the aircraft enters the gust and suddenly finds that it has an apparent flying speed of 21 knots instead of its required 15 knots. The excess speed causes it to rise to a greater height. The increased flying speed not only increases lift but also drag so the aircraft slows down and tries to get back to its correct flying speed of 15 knots. However by this time the aircraft has gained height and now faces a wind speed of probably 8 knots, instead of the original 6 knots, so that the flying speed will still be greater than the original 15 knots and the aircraft will continue to gain height into regions of even greater wind speed.

This is an idealised example but it illustrates the effect of the wind gradient in dynamic lift, and shows that any gust of wind, even at quite low speeds, should cause a man-powered aircraft to climb. Certainly during one flight with Jupiter an altitude of over 10 ft. was achieved that could be attributed directly to the effect of a gust of wind.

Birds take dynamic lift a stage further. They are able to soar within the wind gradient of a steady wind, and so are not restricted to the effect of a gust. The ideal form of dynamic soaring is when the bird flies into the wind and climbs up the wind gradient. At the top of the gradient the bird then turns through 180° and dives down wind, gaining speed so that it can turn back into wind and start climbing again. The bird is taking all the energy required for flight from the wind itself and so could continue this type of soaring indefinitely, or at least whilst the wind lasts.

No branch of aviation has been able to exploit dynamic soaring up till now. Gliders are used at relatively high altitudes and so would not be risked at low altitudes below 50 ft. in order to investigate dynamic lift. However the very fact that dynamic soaring can occur only at low altitudes brings it within the same height range as man-powered flight. Whether man-powered aircraft will be developed that can execute the necessary 180° turns has still to be seen. It would be a major breakthrough for man-powered flight if it did become the only branch of aviation to exploit dynamic soaring.

# References

Ayrton, M., The Testament of Daedalus, Methuen, London, 1962.

Cumming, M., Powerless Ones, Frederick Muller, London, 1966.

Welch, A and L., The story of gliding, John Murray, London.

Lippisch, A.M., Man-powered flight in 1929, Journal of the Royal Aeronautical Society, Vol. 64, No. 595, July 1960, pp. 395-398.

Haessler, H., Man-powered flight in 1935-37 and today, Canadian Aeronautical Journal, March 1961, pp. 89-104. A man has flown by his own power in 1937, Canadian Aeronautical Journal, Dec. 1960, pp. 395-399.

Worley, B., Can man fly? Aeronautics, Feb. 1949.

Raspet, A., Human muscle-powered flight. Soaring, May-June 1952.

Welch, A and L., and Irving F., New soaring pilot, John Murray, London, 1968.

Jensen, V., First controlled hang glider? Soaring, Sept. 1971.

Low and Slow, No. 17, 1972, (address: Self-Soar Association, P.O. Box 1860, Santa Monica, CA 90406, U.S.A.)

Miller, R., The first leap, Low and Slow, No. 2, 1970.

Sherwin, K., Man powered flight, Model and Allied Publications, Hemel Hempstead, 1971.

Schultze, H.G. and Staisny, W., Flug durch muskelkraft, Naturkunde und Technik, Verlag Fritz Knapp, Frankfurt, 1936.

Marsden, A., Williams, D. and Lassiere, A., Southampton's man-powered aircraft, Flight, 23 Nov. 1961, pp. 787-788.

Williams, D.J.M., Man-powered aircraft, Science Journal, Mar. 1966, pp. 74-79.

Piggott, D., letter to the Dunlop Digest, Nov. 1970, p. 17.

Piggott, D., Pedal extremities, Flight, 7 Dec. 1961, p.882.

H.M.P.A. Puffin, Flight, 30 Nov. 1961, p. 843.

Up to date with Puffin II, Flight, 3 Nov. 1966, pp. 757-760.

Moulton, R.G., Aeromodeller Annual, 1966-67.

Der Ikarus von Zeltweg, Hobby, No. 11, 19 May 1968.

Czerwinski, W., Structural trends in the development of man-powered aircraft, Journal of the Royal Aeronautical Society, Vol. 71, No. 673, Jan. 1967, pp. 9-13.

Green, P.K., Man-power project, Shell Aviation News, No. 404, 1972, pp. 2-7.

Pressnell, M.S., Toucan progress report, The Aeronautical Journal, April 1969, p. xxxvi.

Nonweiler, T.R.F., The man-powered aircraft, Journal of the Royal Aeronautical Society, Vol. 62, Oct. 1958, pp. 723-734.

Shenstone, B.S., Engineering aspects of man-powered flight, Journal of the Royal Aeronautical Society, Vol. 64, Aug. 1960, pp. 471-477.

Wilkie, D.R., Man as an aero engine, Journal of the Royal Aeronautical Society, Vol. 64, Aug. 1960, pp. 477-481.

Mitteilungen des muskeflug-institute, Flugsport, Nos. 1-6, 1936-37.

Liebeck, R.H. and Ormsee, A.I., Optimization of airfoils for maximum lift, A.I.A.A. Paper No. 69-739, 1969.

Philips, J.H., Wimpenny, J.C. and Wombwell, J., Piloting aspects of man-powered flight, to be published in the Aeronautical Journal.

Potter, J., The Jupiter Project, The Aeronautical Journal, Vol. 77, 1973, pp. 344-349.

Man-powered flying as a sport, Flight International, 23 Dec. 1971, pp. 1014-1016.

Welch, L., Gliding and man-powered flight, Journal of the Royal Aeronautical Society, Vol. 65, Dec. 1961, pp. 806-814.